Wildlife's Holiday Album

Library of Congress CIP Data: page 157

Wildlife's Holiday Album

An Anthology of Nature Lore
and Holiday Customs

NATIONAL
WILDLIFE
FEDERATION

*A large appetite for holidays,
the ability not only to take them
but to know what to
do with them when taken
is the sign of a robust people.*

Henry James

Contents

The lengthening days of May add golden hours of growth to a hilltop farm in northern Vermont.

Spring

Blossoms grace a greening meadow. Twigs and branches fling open the buds they have saved since fall and wrap themselves in a lace of leaves. Newly hatched insects discover the wonders of flight—and the risks, for the birds are back and hungry. It is spring, and all of nature turns out to welcome the planet's vagrant benefactor, the sun. As the earth leans in its orbit, all her creatures feel the ebb and flow of the sun's energy in tides we call spring, summer, fall, and winter.

Giver of warmth and light and food and life, maker of day and night and season and year, the sun could almost be a god. Through much of the human saga it *was* a god. When it backed away toward the southern horizon each winter, people tried to lure it near again with rite and sacrifice. And when it returned in spring, they welcomed it with festivities that echo in our lives today. Thus it is with all the seasons: they shape our year with customs and holidays, many of them harking to deep antiquity.

But no appointment on nature's calendar gladdens humankind as does the spring. It arrives at no single time. In February the groundhog has its day, stirring briefly from a sleep that is almost death. Birds that fled southward reappear in mating regalia. In March wildflowers parade their rainbow colors. For humans, too, this is a time to strut and preen in the finery of spring. And as man and nature seem once again reborn, faith is reaffirmed in the celebrations of Passover and Easter.

A time of wonder, spring is the year's childhood, bubbling with boundless energy. It brings kites and marbles, baby rabbits, Easter egg hunts, and April Fool jokes. Wise families keep all the holidays, building a store of memories that will green the years of life as they march in ancient cadence, season to season to season.

36.

APRIL

" When daisies red and violets blue   And cuckoo-buds of yellow hue
And ladie's Smocks' all silver white   Do paint the meadows with delight."

The beauty and burgeoning of spring are so fleeting that many persons find it both useful and satisfying to keep a daily log of each new sign of the earth's renewal. It may be little more than a timetable, noting arrivals and departures of robins and violets or the wild geese flying high. But some observers, following the examples of Thoreau and Muir, record their thoughts as well.

A nature diary par excellence was recently discovered on the shelves of an English country house. In this unique book a young naturalist-artist, Edith Holden, had in the spring of 1906 made the entries shown on these pages. Throughout the seasons of that year she reported the changing countryside of her home in Warwickshire.

A Diary for All Seasons

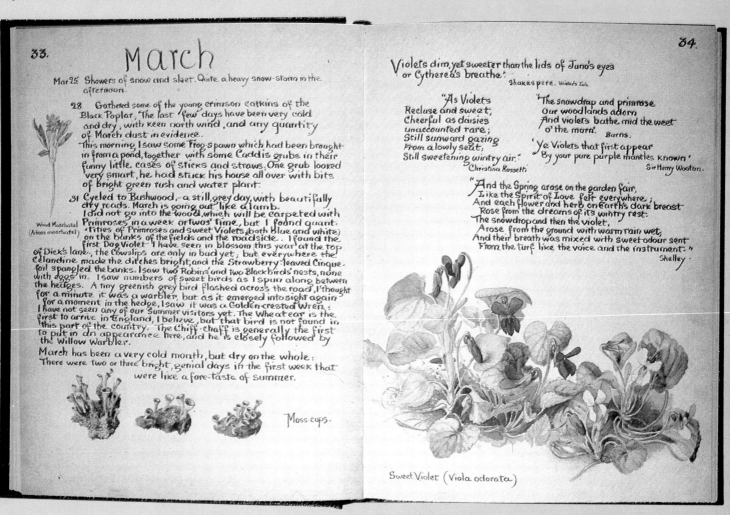

33.

March

Mar 25 Showers of snow and sleet. Quite a heavy snow-storm in the afternoon.

28   Gathered some of the young crimson catkins of the Black Poplar. The last few days have been very cold and dry, with keen north wind, and any quantity of March dust in evidence.
This morning, I saw some Frog-spawn which had been brought in from a pond, together with some Caddis grubs in their funny little cases of sticks and straws. One grub looked very smart, he had stuck his house all over with bits of bright green rush and water plant.

31 Cycled to Bushwood, a still, grey day, with beautifully dry roads. March is going out like a lamb.
I did not go into the wood, which will be carpeted with Primroses in a week or two's time, but I found quantities of Primroses and Sweet Violets (both blue and white) on the banks of the fields and the roadside. I found the first Dog Violet I have seen in blossom this year at the top of Dick's lane, the Cowslips are only in bud yet; but everywhere the Celandine made the ditches bright, and the Strawberry-leaved Cinque-foil spangled the banks. I saw two Robins' and two Blackbirds' nests, none with eggs in. I saw numbers of sweet birds as I spun along between the hedges. A tiny greenish grey bird flashed across the road, I thought for a minute it was a warbler, but as it emerged into sight again for a moment in the hedge, I saw it was a Golden-crested Wren. I have not seen any of our Summer visitors yet. The Wheatear is the first to arrive in England, I believe, but that bird is not found in this part of the country. The Chiff-chaff is generally the first to put in an appearance here, and he is closely followed by the Willow Warbler.

March has been a very cold month, but dry on the whole: There were two or three bright, genial days in the first week that were like a fore-taste of summer.

Wood Moschatel
(Adoxa moschatel)

Moss cups.

34.

Violets dim, yet sweeter than the lids of Juno's eyes or Cytherea's breathe.
Shakespere. Winter's Tale.

"As Violets
Recluse and sweet,
Cheerful as daisies
unaccounted rare,
Still sunward gazing
From a lowly seat,
Still sweetening wintry air."
Christina Rossetti

'The snowdrop and primrose
Our woodlands adorn
And violets bathe mid the weet
o' the morn'.   Burns.

'Ye Violets that first appear
By your pure purple mantles known'
Sir Henry Wooton.

"And the Spring arose on the garden fair,
Like the Spirit of Love felt everywhere;
And each flower and herb on earth's dark breast
Rose from the dreams of its wintry rest.
The snowdrop and then the violet,
Arose from the ground with warm rain wet,
And their breath was mixed with sweet odour sent
From the turf like the voice and the instrument."
Shelley

Sweet Violet (Viola odorata)

Edith Holden died in 1920 and the volume went unnoticed until its discovery and publication in 1977 under the title, *The Country Diary of an Edwardian Lady*. Other excerpts from her remarkable personal journal mark the turning of the seasons on pages 40, 74, and 110 of this anthology.

Of Spring and an Egg

On pine bough and willow limb, in woven basket and ground saucer, hundreds of millions of birds' eggs now lie hidden across the spring-time half of the earth. They vary in shape from the nearly round egg of the screech owl to the pear-shape of the plover; in size from the ponderous two-pound egg of the ostrich to the three-hundredth-of-an-ounce egg of the hummingbird. But all have two things in common: they started as a beautiful gold-and-crystal cell within the female, and they maintain a dynamic, unbroken and endless pattern that has existed since the beginning of bird history.

A newly hatched female, upon cracking out of her shell, has already within her body a supply of tiny, pinpoint-sized eggs, many more than she will lay in her lifetime!

Both the process and the timing of egg formation inside the female is quite precise—the same for domestic and wild birds. An egg starts out as a single cell, a spark of life. Still in the mother's body, it grows in size and complexity as layers of yolk, albumen, membrane and shell are laid around it. But it remains a single cell. It may or may not be fertilized by a male sperm in the process of its formation. If it is, it still must wait until it has been laid and incubated by the mother before a chick begins to form.

In picking an arbitrary starting point in the bird-and-egg cycle, scientists usually begin when the first coating of yolk is laid around a germ cell in the young chick. Thousands of closely timed microscopic studies reveal that this happens when the chick is at least two months old. Moreover, they show that an egg yolk is made up of several rings of varying shades of yellow.

The formation of the final layer requires the presence of a male bird to set it off. His just being there in a spring-time tree triggers a hormonal change in the now mature female that creates the final layer. Most wild birds cannot lay if there is no mate. This is not true of domestic birds—barnyard chickens, ducks, and pigeons can lay unfertilized eggs throughout their productive lives. Poultrymen keep breeder hens and roosters too, of course, to perpetuate the species; but the egg you have for breakfast has probably been laid without prompting by a male. The record holder in this area is a leghorn chicken who laid 1,515 in eight years, and she never saw a rooster in her life.

The next activity in a bird's egg-laying is dramatic. With its lustrous yolk sac completed, the egg ruptures from its mooring and falls into the oviduct. In wild birds this event is also triggered by the male—his courtship dances and displays whirl the chemicals in the female and touch off the plunge. These male dances are often bold and dashing. The woodcock, for instance, flies high in the air, then flutters back, straight toward the earth. The pheasant male jabs the ground and fans his tail into a heart-shaped shield. The blue bird of paradise hangs upside down and shakes his iridescent plumes into a blue mist. The American egret makes a show of his aigrettes (display feathers) and gives his mate a present of a stick. Each species has a different expression of affection, but they all achieve the same end.

Then mating takes place, and as the free egg proceeds down the funnel-like oviduct it encounters a male sperm. A special structure in the sperm disintegrates and releases enzymes that break down the outer membranes of the egg. As a result, the sperm is able to penetrate the egg and fertilize it.

Now comes the stopwatch phase of embryological research, for immediately after fertilization the egg goes on a schedule that is quite predictable. It stops in the oviduct for about 20 minutes while it gathers albumen, or white. Like the yolk, the albumen is a series of layers. The first is a thin covering. The second is dense, elastic and tough, a shock absorber to protect the spark of life in the center from the plunge to the nest and the tumbling it gets during incubation.

The egg moves on, spiraling now as it goes downward through the oviduct. The spiral motion squeezes a very light, watery fluid out of the second layer of albumen to form a new one in which the yolk floats, orienting itself with gravity. The original tiny cell (which is the white speck you sometimes see in a cracked fresh egg) buoys to the top.

The spiraling serves another pur-

pose—it twists the albumen at either end into a "rope," the two visible milky threads that every housewife recognizes. These ropes play an important role by keeping the yolk in the center of the egg. The ropes later break in the incubation stage, so the mother must rotate the egg to keep the yolk from settling to one side.

The proportion of yolk to albumen is not the same in all eggs. A duckling or young plover remains in its egg until it is ready to run around and find food on its own when it hatches. This greater development takes longer and requires more food in the form of yolk. A wren, on the other hand, hatches helpless and needs ten or more days of parental care. Thus a wren's egg has less yolk, more albumen.

Next on the schedule is the formation of the two snow-white sheets of tough membranes that are found under the shell of the breakfast egg. This takes about an hour and ten minutes. Then the egg drops into the shell-secreting area of the oviduct and remains there for about 20 hours while the shell accumulates in four porous layers.

During the last few hours of shell secretion the egg is colored. There are approximately 9,000 species of birds in the world, many with distinctively marked or colored eggs. The color and markings of the shells are immutable.

The entire process of making an egg after fertilization takes just about 24 hours. The schedule is tight, but there is a degree of elasticity in this final

A white ibis breaks out of the egg. The tiny bird cracked the shell by rubbing it with its egg-tooth, the white bump on the tip of its upper beak.

stage. The actual laying can be delayed—if the mother happens to be away from the nest when the schedule is done, she can hold it back for several hours. The laying time also varies from species to species. A domestic hen, protected for thousands of years against enemies, spends a leisurely two hours on the nest whereas a wild quail, preyed upon by hawk and fox, spends a hasty three to ten minutes. But the world over, eggs are laid only during daylight hours. The majority of eggs are laid between sunup and noon. At sunset all egg-laying stops.

At the time a bird egg is laid, it is covered by a glistening film, which soon hardens. Then the fertilized egg waits for warmth. Air is entering the pores in the shell, and a breathing pocket is forming at the blunt end. Here, after incubation begins, the chick's head will lie.

Now the egg is finished. The mother bird will lay more until she has filled her quota. Then the eggs in her nest start her on a new schedule of brooding and turning. However, some birds won't start to incubate until the right number of eggs lie in the nest. A female flicker, for instance, must sense four before she is triggered to brood. An ornithologist who removed one egg a day from a flicker's nest so detained the female that she laid 71 before she gave up.

It is the heat of the mother's body that triggers the explosion of life within the egg—suddenly when the temperature at the center reaches 99.5 degrees the cell development begins again. On and on the chain reaction goes until within the silent shell there are lungs, a heart, liver, eyes, all the exquisite organs of a living chick.

Last Easter, in order to observe this miracle close up, I purchased six fertile bobwhite eggs and a globe-shaped plastic incubator from a quail farm. I placed the eggs in the incubator and turned on a 7-watt Christmas tree bulb that brought the heat to 99.5 degrees and held it there.

But it was the 23rd, the hatching day, that I waited for. On that day, once an hour, I hovered over the incubator. Then, before my eyes, a crack shattered the side of one egg like the beginning of a miniscule volcano. I lifted the egg and heard a voice within—thin, high, fragile. I put it down and watched off and on during the night as bits of shell were broken in a circle at the big end.

At noon, when the sun illuminated the yellow-green buds of the apple tree and the white crocuses on the lawn, the first tiny bird burst out of the shell into spring.

It rested for several hours while, one after the other, a brother and a sister cracked out of their shells; then dry, fluffy and tantalizing, it got up on its feet as though in a hurry to keep some mystical appointment with the eternal life it harbored.

Jean George

Who Laid the Eggs?

1. Screech Owl

E ach of these birds would have no trouble picking out its own eggs from among those shown below. But can you match them up correctly? Before you read the answers (printed upside down below), here are a few tips.

Small eggs are usually laid by small birds. Pale colored eggs are more likely to belong to a cavity-nesting bird than to one that uses an open nest. If there are ten or more eggs in a clutch (the total number laid for hatching at one time), they were probably laid by a chicken-like bird. But remember this: even an ornithologist cannot always be positive in identifying eggs unless he sees the mother bird on the nest.

(Answers: (1-D, 2-A, 3-C, 4-F, 5-E, 6-B)

4. Hooded Warbler

B. Clue: Pennsylvania state birds will hatch from these eggs.

A. Clue: A small game bird whose wings whistle when it flies laid these eggs.

C. Clue: These brown-spotted eggs contrast with their brightly colored male parent.

2. *Woodcock*

3. *Scarlet Tanager*

5. *Eastern Bluebird*

6. *Ruffed Grouse*

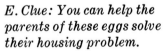

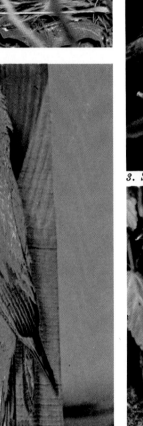

E. Clue: You can help the parents of these eggs solve their housing problem.

F. Clue: The tiny male bird responsible for these eggs wears a winter hat in summer.

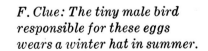

D. Clue: Parents of these eggs may be brown or gray, and are strangers to the day.

The Customs of Easter

Squealing, stumbling, blinking sleep from their eyes in the chill Hungarian dawn, the young girls are pushed and pulled by village youths toward a fate they have expected all year. Here's the river bank; one good shove and—splash!

And now, how will these dampened damsels repay the grinning swains standing warm and dry on the bank? With gifts of eggs, breads, even a spot of brandy—for in the folk wisdom of this ancient rite, the boys of old Hungary have ensured that the girls will become good wives.

Though time has tamed the rough old ritual, Hungarian boys still splash the girls from buckets, bottles, or a nearby well on *Locsolkodas*—Dousing Day, the Monday after Easter.

Dousing Day has no Christian root, no Easter equivalent. It stems directly from pagan rites of spring. In every cranny of the Christian world, the customs of Easter and the rituals of spring are so intertwined that it is often impossible to sort one from the other. And who would want to? For Easter says to the human spirit what springtime says to the winter-weary world. Each is faith rewarded, life renewed, a year begun. Easter could only happen in the spring.

For several centuries after the first Easter morning, clerics argued over when and how its date should be fixed. Finally, in solemn council, they decided to let the sun and moon determine the day—as the two had always decided the date of Passover, the great Jewish holy day that Jesus and his disciples celebrated at supper the night before he was crucified. The first full moon on or after March 21, the vernal equinox when day equals night, fixes Easter as the very next Sunday. Thus our star and satellite conspire to give us a chilly Easter as early as March 22 or a balmy one as late as April 25.

Early or late, chilly or not, the sun on Easter morning peers over hills and plains at countless gatherings of upturned faces—just as it did when pagans began the custom of sunrise services long centuries ago. Catching the first rays of sunrise they send back a chorus of joy: "Christ the Lord is risen today, Alleluia!"

Out of the sunrise may have come the very name of Easter—and with it the first hippity-hoppings of that ubiquitous season symbol, the Easter Bunny. Some hear in "Easter" an echo of Eos, the maiden who personified the dawn in the myths of ancient Greece. Others, beginning with England's great eighth-century scholar, the Venerable Bede, catch a fleeting whisper of Eostre, an old Teutonic goddess of spring. Little is known of this pagan deity, and even less of why she chose for her sacred animal the spring hare. But there he is, shadowy ears flopping through the mists of antiquity. Indeed, his pedigree may reach back far beyond hers. For ancient Egyptians linked the hare with the moon, and when early Christians linked the moon with Easter they may have unwittingly taken aboard a furry stowaway.

Eostre, the old Germanic legends say, created the very first hare by fashioning it from a bird. Once a year, on the occasion of her spring festival, the grateful hare would express its thanks by laying eggs. Eostre's sun has long since set, but as Easter's rose the ancient legend was reborn with it. Throughout Christendom there are no stronger folk-symbols of spring and Easter than the fecund Easter Bunny and the life-renewing egg.

Today, both are cast in chocolate, printed on greeting cards, feted in song, and offered up to holiday shoppers in myriad manifestations. But the rabbit is an upstart compared to the egg, an enduring symbol of fertility and

Forerunners of the Easter egg hunt, egg games of yesteryear live on in drawings a century old. A young Swiss (below) races to gather up 100 eggs before a competitor sprints to a goal and back. Attempts to trip him are part of the game. More difficult is the dance of the whirling Bengal damsel (opposite) who slips 24 unbroken eggs from basket to string halo and back without missing a beat.

Ukrainian Easter egg artists turn to nature for symbols to adorn their gem-like pysanki: a stag for health, a sunburst for luck, flowers for love, birds for wishes soon to come true. Each hollow masterpiece may take a day's work and become an heirloom. The Easter Bunny's efforts, as portrayed here on 1912 postal greeting cards, are no match.

renewal in most of the cultures of mankind. Ancient Romans, Greeks, Persians, Chinese, Babylonians—all gave eggs as gifts at springtime. From their day to ours, the egg has inspired rites and customs in bewildering variety.

A hare that could lay eggs would be a rare hare indeed, and rarer still to produce them in colors. So the human imagination supplies what nature cannot. The decoration of Easter eggs has enthralled and busied celebrants since at least the 15th century and possibly long before that. The art is even older than the holiday; in 900 B.C. the Chinese were giving each other red-painted eggs during their festival of spring.

Through the centuries, Easter egg decoration has become an exuberant art. Colors that once came from spinach leaves, onion peels, flower petals, and even old rags now come from commercial dyes in a limitless rainbow of hues. Messages are inscribed with grease pencils; pictures are applied with decals. Sometimes the egg's content is blown out through a pinhole; the fragile shell is then adorned and hung with others on an indoor tree. In Eastern Europe, eggs become masterpieces in the hands of artists who painstakingly work out intricate designs.

No such artistry rewards the pace-eggers of northern England. But still these youngsters make their rounds every Easter, like trick-or-treating Halloweeners, begging colored eggs from door to door as they vow in song that "we'll come no more a-pace-egging until another year." "Pace" comes from the old word for Easter, "paschal,"

itself an echo of the ancient Hebrew word for Passover.

Many countries have enjoyed some version of the English "egg-shackling." The premise of the game is that my hard-boiled egg can beat yours. So you grip yours tightly in a fist, I grip mine, and—whack! The winner gets the loser's cracked egg and a shot at the next contender's.

The eggshell's fragility inspired another, well-traveled custom. Egg-rolling harks to Norway and Germany, where the object is to roll a hard-boiled egg down a slope without cracking its shell. Depending on locale, outdistancing the competition wins a variety of rewards—good luck, the prospect of an early marriage, even the losers' eggs. In Dolley Madison's day the idea rolled across the Atlantic and came to rest on the White House lawn. Except in time of war, on Easter Monday the eggs of thousands of children have gone lolloping down the greensward ever since.

Through the merriment of Easter, children can share in a sacred event whose meaning and message they cannot yet fully grasp. When I was a tad in small-town Connecticut, I understood little of such matters as resurrection and the Trinity. But I knew beyond doubt that the Easter Bunny by dark of night would seek out the shoe I had carefully placed under my bed—and carefully cleaned out first. By Easter morning the old shoe that had pedaled bikes, slid into second, and kicked countless tin cans down the sidewalk had been magically transformed into an elfin ark, lined with green cellophane grass and filled with a clutch of jelly beans and eggs dyed in wondrous swirls and patterns. And in the middle, sculpted in chocolate that I couldn't bring myself to bite into for weeks, stood the Easter Bunny, as real as Santa Claus. All over the world, other kids were finding similar treats in nests in the grass, in baskets, and in every nook their elders could think of.

Now with the perspective of years, I walk through the spring woods and pluck a posy for Eostre, creator of the Easter Bunny. In spring and Easter I see deeper meanings. But before wisdom dawns and faith matures, a child can share in the joys of a joy-filled season through the ageless customs of Easter.

David F. Robinson

It's spring and the earth is dressed up in its brightest colors for the occasion. Maybe you'll want to do a little decorating yourself. What about turning eggs into gaily colored animals for a miniature zoo? You probably already have most of what you need: eggs, egg dye or paint, a darning needle or ice pick, scissors, a felt tip pen, several colors of construction paper, crayons, white glue, and a little imagination.

Before coloring the eggs, hard boil them or blow out their contents. Boiled eggs kept at room temperature stay fresh enough to eat for three or four days. (Be sure to use an edible dye.) In the refrigerator, they last for 10 days. Of course blown eggs never spoil, but they are easily broken.

To blow an egg, use the darning needle or ice pick to poke a small hole at one end of the egg and another, smaller one at the opposite end. Be sure to push the pick all the way through the shell and into the yolk itself. Hold the egg over a cup, and blow into the smaller hole with steady breaths until the egg is empty. Rinse the egg and let it dry. Now you're ready for the real fun—decorating!

Easter Egg Zoo

Egg Bunny
Materials: hardboiled or blown egg; Easter egg dye or acrylic or enamel paint; several colors of construction paper; cotton ball; white glue.

Method: Cut ears, eyes, and whiskers from paper, and glue to the large rounded end of the egg to make the face. Glue on cotton ball for tail.

Egg Bird
Materials: blown egg; Easter egg dye or acrylic or enamel paint; ice pick or needle; two colors of construction paper; felt tip pen; white glue.

Method: Puncture and enlarge a hole on each side of egg for wings. For tail, enlarge one of holes used for blowing. Fold three pieces of paper ($2\frac{3}{4}$" x 8") into fine pleats. Tightly hold pleats together at one end and insert wings and tail into place. Cut out triangular beak and glue to egg. With a felt pen, draw eyes on small circles of paper and glue to egg.

Egg Butterfly
Materials: hardboiled or blown egg; Easter egg dye or enamel or acrylic paint; black crayon; several colors of construction paper; white glue.

Method: Cut out wings and figure-eight body shape and color designs onto them with crayon. Glue wings and body to egg. Cut out antennae, curl ends, and glue onto egg.

Impatient Spring

Ordinarily, our old maple tree is fairly well behaved. So I was quite unprepared on that February day when it hissed at me. "Ps-s-s-t!" it said.

Puzzled, I stared at it. Now I could see that something was taking place. Half a dozen chickadees were attacking a huge flake of bark on the trunk. I waded through the snow to the maple, and in those few feet I walked from winter into spring.

The part of the trunk that attracted the chickadees was broadside to the rays of the morning sun. Warmed by this heat, hundreds of cluster flies had stirred from their winter bed beneath the bark, and now they were pushing and shoving their way out into the sunshine. Every so often one would buzz its wings briefly. The loose bark, acting as a sounding board, magnified the noise: ps-s-s-t!

The chickadees, of course, were giving them a hungry welcome. They pecked away at the emerging flies, enjoying this six-legged addition to their routine handout of suet and sunflower seeds.

For nearly two hours the banquet continued. Then the sun moved, abandoning the tree trunk. With the coming of shade, the flies slipped back into winter. And the chickadees returned to the bird feeder.

Such little tastes of spring make it hard to say, really, when the new season actually does begin. The calendar gives one date. The groundhog and his shadow foretell another. Countless little clues—like flies that cannot wait—give still others.

One of the first spring flowers, for instance, may have already been waiting for those same buzzing flies. And "waiting" is just the word, for early spring insects may be vital to its existence. That flower is the peculiar purple-striped cup of the skunk cabbage,

Brash daffodils challenge winter's last stand as other signs of spring appear: the early waking skunk and its odiferous namesake, the skunk cabbage; a mourning cloak butterfly basking in new warmth; and a pregnant fox that mated in January to raise her pups in the April sun.

first cousin of the jack-in-the-pulpit and of the philodendron on your windowsill. Some time in late winter, a hidden impulse triggers the skunk cabbage into life. The roots, buried six inches or more beneath the soil along a stream or marsh, begin to convert their stored food into energy. Forcing its way through frost and snow, the growing bud surges upward.

Having risen above ground, the skunk cabbage now proceeds to demonstrate how it got its name—*Sym-plocarpus foetidus*, "the plant that smells." Little glands in the tissues produce a powerful odor, supposedly reminiscent of skunk, although to me it's more like a garbage heap. Wafted by the breeze, the odor calls flies, restless beetles and other wakening insects. Landing on the plant's pollen-laden center, they fertilize the curious blossom, giving it a running start on spring while less venturesome flowers are still underground.

The same moist ground that bears skunk cabbage may yield other spring hopefuls. Walk near almost any brook or stream on a mild winter day. The chances are you will find a winter stone fly—a half-inch creature with wings it seldom uses—nearing the end of its existence. For months it has been a flattened nymph clinging to the bottom of the stream. Now, it pokes its way up through the grasses and debris at the river's edge, seeking another of its kind. If it is successful, it may mate, lay its eggs, and die before the ice has left the river.

The February sun is a heat lamp to many creatures besides the stone fly: spiders that creep over the surface of the snow as if in a dream; little brown caterpillars called from their grass-roots slumbers; wingless crane flies walking on their long legs. You may see gnats that fly in feeble circles until a cold draft hits them and they stall out. Brown miller moths work up enough energy to flit across an opening in the woods; the sugarmaker will call them "sap moths" when they get into his buckets a few weeks later.

You might even be treated to the improbable sight of a butterfly twinkling over the snow. The mourning cloak, decked in heat-absorbent brown, red and blue, with cream-bordered wings, has stirred from its hollow tree. Now it flits to a broken maple twig and samples a drop of sap.

As soon as the sun wanes, it goes back to its tree house.

An hour after your woodland stroll, each of your footprints in the snow may be carpeted by thousands of snow fleas. This odd insect is about the size and color of a speck of pepper. It acts about as a speck of pepper might, too, if that spicy condiment should come to life. Cocked beneath the snow flea's abdomen is a taut little spring, held in place by a trigger. When the trigger is released, the tiny insect is catapulted into the air. Hence its other common name, "springtail." Possibly the compressed snow allows more light to seep down, calling them up for a spring frolic.

As the days lengthen, more harbingers appear. The skunk, stirring at night from its underground den, pokes around in search of venturesome insects, old apples, or—opportunist that it is—a member of the opposite sex.

Gifted with much the same outlook on life, the raccoon also rouses itself to meet spring in advance. You can find its tracks, looking like the prints of baby's feet (hind tracks) plus little hands (front tracks) in the snow. Like the skunk, the 'coon is not fussy about what it eats. Often the first hint you get that the ringtailed little burglar has awakened is the clatter of your garbage-pail cover being knocked off in the dark.

Out in the woods the black bear yawns and stretches. Having stuffed its innards with pine needles and other debris last fall, it feels no need for food yet. It takes a little walk anyway. Then it returns for a few more weeks of slumber, like a man who wakens and resets the alarm clock for 40 more winks.

Even hungry, four-footed nibblers —especially the rabbits and deer—get

a new lease on life as melting snow uncovers new twigs and buds. Rabbits leave the ends of twigs cut on a slant, because they have to tilt their heads to slice with those buck teeth. Deer, having no uppers in front, twist their food from the branch, leaving the twigs frayed and splintered.

The first stirrings of spring have sounds of their own, too. It is the time for seeking a mate, and such an important occasion deserves to be announced. As early as February, the quiet of my snowy woods may be shattered by the drumming of a downy woodpecker. This feathered riveter advertises his availability by finding a hollow tree with just the right resonance and whacking away.

Every bit as meaningful to the ears for which they are intended are the courtship calls of other creatures: the moonlight yip of the red fox, the unearthly yowl of the bobcat, the first rhythmic thumpings of the rabbit as it drums its hind feet to announce to prospective mates that the time has nearly come to start living up to their reputation.

Then, too, there's the spring song of the chickadee. All fall and early winter the black-and-white little waif has said his name over and over as he searched every crack for insects or hammered away at goldenrod galls for the grub that each contains. Now, apparently cheered by the lengthening days, he bursts out in a new song: a high, sweet, two-note whistle, "Spring . . . soon. Spring . . . soon."

There are dozens—hundreds—of other little signs telling us that, even while it looks as if we're in another ice age, winter is really being pushed aside by spring. Even though the robin gets the first worm, it's really no early bird at all.

Ronald Rood

Wild Love

WHAM! Clashing antlers of young bull elk advertise their struggle for dominance in the herd. The winner takes all, including the best foraging ground and the pick of the cows during fall rutting season. The loser either successfully defends a less desirable territory or remains virginal. Such struggles ensure that only the strongest and healthiest mate.

Screening out the weaklings is also a function of the vigorous dance of India's sarus cranes. Pairs, sometimes whole flocks, of these spectacular birds jump as high as 10 to 12 feet into the balmy air and wave and bob their heads in a prelude to mating. Both male and female cranes are sexually aggressive, behavior that contrasts sharply with the peafowl family. The peacock has to do all the work. He sometimes must strut his magnificent train of 5-foot tail feathers in front of the peahen several times before she deigns to look up from her feeding. At the height of his courtship performance, the peacock shrieks horrifically and then settles back before starting all over again.

Spring has returned to the land, arousing in wildlife the urge to court and mate, to bear the young that replenish the species. Survival is the ultimate goal of all wildlife, and to survive means to reproduce.

Each animal species gives birth to its young when conditions are most favorable to their survival. In the northern hemisphere that is usually in the spring, when longer, warmer days spread a banquet of plants and insects to fill hungry new mouths. Then summer's cornucopia of food builds the young into the sturdy creatures they must become to survive their first winter.

Wild love is not as simple as it may seem. At times, it is dangerous, bringing pain, injury, even death to the male. He usually defends his breeding territory by making threats, but serious battles do erupt. Thick-horned mountain rams occasionally kill their opponents during rutting season. Female praying mantises often bite off the heads of their suitors during copulation, and the drone honey-bee dies in mid-flight after fertilizing the queen.

Even when mating is not dangerous, it often is difficult, especially among animals who must search for partners. Animals usually mate only with others of their own kind. For butterflies and other small, widely distributed species, just finding a mate is like finding a needle in a haystack. Species in which the male and female look alike or closely resemble another species rely on very subtle recognition signals. Even when males and females are distinctive and easily found, they must find ways to communicate their readiness to mate. To breed in spite of all the haz-

Animal mating ranges from the conspicuous to the secretive, the commonplace to the bizarre. Some butterflies alight, and during coupling—perhaps several hours—stand so still they elude predators. Dragonflies may spend days in the conjugal tryst, flying in tandem to guard the female from other males. Contrary to appearances, frogs do not copulate. The male, on top, grasps the female and together they arch their backs, she dispelling eggs and he the fertilizing sperm. Cattle egrets, like most birds, come together only briefly. But not snails. Hermaphroditic, each partner fertilizes the other after an hour of courtship in which each snail shoots into the other a tiny, chalk-like "love" dart.

ards and difficulties, animals have evolved courtship displays and rituals that are amazingly complex combinations of sounds, movements and postures, colors, and smells.

Males' assertive growls, grunts, bellows, bugles, and songs not only express the mounting tensions of the mating season but signal all females within earshot that they are wanted. When female songbirds respond, the birds pair off and sing to each other to strengthen the bond that will lead to their mating and nesting. The persistent, raucous "songs" of grasshoppers, crickets, and cicadas attract females and then help synchronize their drives to mate. The loud croaks of male frogs signal their location and announce their sexual desires. Even some fish use sounds in courtship. Cod make a grunting noise and male satinfin shiners make a "knocking" noise in response to females that enter their territories.

Once potential partners have come close enough to see each other, the female is further attracted by the threatening behavior of the male. A dominant bull elk testily displaying his horns or shredding a small tree intimidates

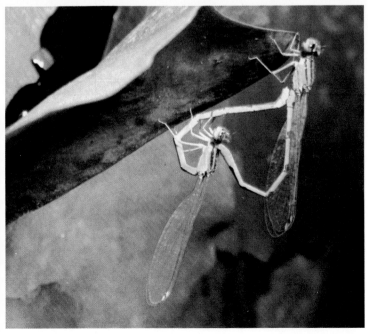

other bulls and causes a female coming into heat to act submissively so she can join his harem. Songbirds conspicuously raise their bills skyward, puff up their feathers, and assume threatening poses to keep away other males and attract receptive females. Playful acts, too, may have double meaning. All winter long, both male and female cranes playfully dance by bowing, jumping, running in circles, and flinging sticks into the air; but when spring comes, these same dances become invitations to mate.

Bright colors and feather finery showily displayed—one might say flaunted—are, to human eyes, one of the more delightful aspects of courtship behavior. The peacock's iridescent blue, green, and bronze feathers are present year round, but they are paraded with finesse in courting season. Modestly showing the dull rear-side of his tail feathers, the peacock sidles up to the peahen. Suddenly, he jerks himself around, seductively flashing and quivering the gorgeously colored side of his fan. How could any female ignore such flattery for long? Normally, cattle egrets have all-white feathers and yellow eyes. But in spring, feathers on their heads, breasts, and backs turn a buff color and eyes become a stimulating red. Before the mating season, the bellies of male three-spined stickleback fish change from camouflage green to a brilliant red that advertises their nestbuilding to females.

Butterflies, too, use brilliant colors to attract partners, but moths, operating in the dark, employ smells. When a female moth is ready to mate, glands on her abdomen secrete a potent odor that is wafted by air currents created by her wings. This unique perfume guides males to her—from miles around. Smells also play a large role in the courtship of mammals. Females in heat attract males by emitting scents from their genital areas. The odor alerts the male, and he follows her until she is ready to mate.

Courting and mating arrangements among animals may seem unnecessarily complex or frivolously beautiful, but they are really nature's ultimate demonstration of practicality and necessity. Their fantasic diversity is eloquent testimony to Nature's decree to carry on.

Howard Robinson

Mating done, family responsibilities begin. Both flamingo parents guard their chick and feed it predigested food for two weeks. Dall sheep ewes nurse their lambs for several months. Mother opossum, by carrying her litter for three months, teaches them to hunt, and to fight—by bluffing or by playing dead. En route they may crawl from their backside perch into her pouch to nurse.

April Showers

On a cold twilight in winter, a chickadee on its way home to sleep cached a wheat seed in the apple tree near my window. He never returned for it. Rain and snow fell, the sun warmed it and the wind cooled it.

Finally, one day in April, a warm shower pooled in the crotch where it lay. Toward evening, I glanced at the wheat grain. Then I leaned out the window. For a pale root tip had burst the seed coat, and I marveled that one April shower could start life, high in that soilless garden. I brought the seedling into the house and potted it to remind myself that all over the northern half of the globe billions of seeds like this one were germinating and would soon send shoots above ground to brighten the earth.

The next day, still awed by the rain and the seedling, I asked a plant expert, "Just what is so special about an April shower?"

"The April shower is the first water to touch the seeds when the ground is warm enough to renew life," he replied. From an astrophysicist I learned that the rain is sun-distilled water, almost pure—but only "al-most." Putting out his hand into a sudden April shower and bringing it back glittering with raindrops, he said, "I have just caught a handful of meteors. The atmosphere is filled with tiny flecks of iron from outer space. When they pass through a raincloud they become one of several catalysts for rainmaking. Vapor snatches them. The result: a raindrop with a meteor for a heart."

Since that day, I think of raindrops as iron messengers verifying that there are galaxies beyond galaxies, beyond worlds.

The raindrops hurtling into the ground in April pick up soluble minerals that will help give life to thirsty growth. Seeping down into the earth, raindrops find the surfaces of seeds, for water loves to cling to dry surfaces. And some seeds, for their part, have remarkable ability to take in moisture, through and around cells in the coat. I usually pop some beans into a plate of April rainwater and place it on the kitchen table so we all can see what happens on a rainy day in the darkness of the earth. My daughter watched a bean so long she actually saw it fill, "like a toy balloon." Inside the seed coat the rainwater swells the protein, re-establishes cell membranes, and sets the growth process in motion.

To watch my daffodil roots absorb rainwater and grow, I pushed a piece of glass into the earth beside the bulb and dug back the soil. After each April shower I traced the roots on the glass with a wax pencil. There were days when the roots grew an inch.

Once the rainwater has seeped into the roots, it shinnies up the plant by capillary attraction. But there is another, more spectacular water elevator: heat. A botanist at the University of Michigan made this dramatically clear to me. He snipped off a leafy house plant—a geranium—and put its stem in a bottle of red ink. The ink crept slowly up the stem, as mercury does in a thermometer. "But now watch," the botanist said. He placed the plant and ink under an electric light. The heat evaporated the moisture on the leaf surface and the red ink shot up, two inches per minute. "That's what the sun does," he said.

Trees have still another way of getting water. Most, in April, have no leaves to evaporate and pull, and cap-illary attraction is hardly strong enough to lift water 100 feet into the sky. However, the difference between the air pressure on the surface of the ground and on the top of the tree, combined with root pressure, is pump enough for a forest. The weight at the bottom pushes the water, just as pressing down on the milk in a glass sends it up the straw.

The April shower can be as important to some animals as to plants. Last spring it was not until after a long, warm April shower that a chipmunk ended his hibernation under the stone wall in our garden. When he emerged, his body was thin, his face gaunt. I thought he must be starving and threw oatmeal on the ground. He ignored it and hurried to a stone that held a pot of water. The chipmunk lowered his head and drank for four minutes without stopping, fairly swelling like a bean.

Some animals know how to take advantage of the rain. I remember a fox that denned on the hill behind our cabin in New York. By the time April came she had five kits, and early one morning I saw this vixen step into the rain and go to the low meadow by the stream that overflows in every spring rain. The tunnels of the meadow were flooded, and the mice were easy prey as they sought shelter in hummocks and under leaves. With a mouthful of morsels for her kits, she circled back to her den.

I lifted my field glasses and laughed to see that I shared something with that fox. Even as my children and I pressed against the window, watching the buds green, the fox lay at the entrance of her den, nose on paws, watching the soft April shower. Her kits snuggled against her. Were they, I wondered, like my youngsters, sleepily listening to the drip and splash of spring?

Jean George

Water droplets on a blade of grass multiply images of life awakened by earlier rains. At dawn, these tiny orbs become convex focusing lenses, glittering like jewels with the reflection of the golden groundsel blooming below. Photographer Hans Pfletschinger used bellows, reversed 50 mm. macro lens, extension tubes, and electronic flash to get the shot.

Gardening With Wild Flowers

Canada Lily

Remember the delight of discovering wild flowers on an outdoor excursion during the first warm days of spring? Great expanses of colorful blossoms, and here and there a single shy native bloom almost hidden from view? If you have a small vacant corner in your backyard, you can have some of that beauty at home.

Your wild-flower gardening adventure should begin with analyzing your soil and planting site and consulting wild-flower catalogs for plants that will thrive in it. Of course you may be able to transplant some wildlings from areas about to be disrupted by lumbering, road building, or other construction activity. You may even be able to collect from other sites where wild flowers are abundant *if your state law permits it, and you have the landowner's permission.*

Because wild flowers grow naturally without a gardener's attention, some folks think all you need to do is dig a hole, transplant, and forget them. Not true! To give these sometimes exacting plants every possible encouragement, prepare sites in advance and plant as soon as possible after collecting. Plants can be moved in any season if their roots are kept well balled in their own soil. They require only normal shade and water.

However, if plants cannot be replanted within a few hours, select small specimens, cut off all flowers and some foliage, shake the soil from the roots, and put the plants in a plastic bag without added moisture. Seal bags and keep out of the sun in a cool place. As soon as you can, replant the barerooted plants in moist, sandy soil to stimulate new root growth before permanent planting.

Even when you start your garden with seeds, care is needed. For mass plantings it is generally futile merely to scatter seeds. Prepare a fine seed bed, plant the seeds, gently cover, then keep the soil moist until they sprout.

Not all wild flowers will grow well together at the same site because their demands for light, moisture, soil texture, and acidity vary widely. Fortunately, most plants thrive in a neutral soil if texture, light, and moisture are adequate. And it is quite possible to meet the particular demands of most other wild flowers by preparing small, made-to-order areas within

Wood Anemone

Jack-in-the-Pulpit

Fringed Gentian

your garden. If your soil is alkaline or neutral, for example, you may make a small area of it acid by using rocks or logs to raise it a few inches above the rest. Here, by adding acid peat, pine and hemlock needles, or chemical soil acidifiers, you may host the acid-loving plants, such as trailing arbutus, bunchberry, and wintergreen.

For plants which need added moisture, a small excavation lined with plastic and filled with moisture-retaining humus soil will perform wonders. An old washtub, sink, or bathtub imbedded in the ground so its rim does not show can provide a niche for plants which normally demand sites such as bogs, pine barrens, gravelly moraines, or deep, rich acid duffs.

Most woodland plants like soil with a high humus content. Duff, formed by decomposition of fallen leaves and needles, forms an open soil and helps hold moisture. But most forest soils are not very fertile, so the judicious addition of balanced organic fertilizers and a light top dressing of phosphate will give extra vigor and more blooms to all woodland wild flowers.

Different types of plants need varying amounts of light. Few will flourish in the constant dense shade of evergreens. Spring bloomers in deciduous forests enjoy the canopy of leafy shade in the summer after they have flowered in the stronger light before the tree leaves expand in the spring. Most woodland wild flowers will grow more vigorously with more light than they had in the wild—if not parched by too much summer sun.

Rocks in the woodland garden not only add to its beauty, but provide among them pockets where deep deposits of humus can accumulate. Close to the base of rocks, moisture is retained and searched out by the roots of wild flowers. It is in such sites that we commonly find Dutchman's-breeches, trilliums, anemones, mayapples and ferns.

Design your garden to include some flowers which bloom later in the season. Canada lily, the snake-roots, red catchfly, and the bottle gentian are among these late bloomers. The fruits of the blue cohosh, baneberries, Solomon's seals and Jack-in-the-pulpits will also provide a colorful array in the summer and autumn months.

Varied textures and shapes of leaves add a beguiling charm. Ferns add grace and rich color. Careful placement of groups of Solomon's seal with its arching stems, and of mayapple with its great umbrella leaves makes a most pleasing design.

Many wild flowers are deciduous, and some, like the spring beauties and the dicentras, are very transitory, not only losing their foliage, but disappearing below ground early in the season. To avoid the bare ground look that follows, you can plant them among wide swatches of ground-covering plants with evergreen foliage, such as partridgeberry, wintergreen, pipsissewa, foamflower, and the polypody and Christmas ferns.

Wild-flower gardening is admittedly a challenge, but the important thing is to make a start. Though no longer totally wild and free, in the garden your wild flowers will bloom for the enjoyment of future generations.

Lincoln Foster

Spring Beauty

Great white trillium, wild blue phlox, foamflower, and wild ginger adorn a garden path in this man-made wildflower sanctuary in Westport, Connecticut. Almost 20 years ago, when the garden was designed, resident oak and evergreen trees provided humus-filled soil for the myriad species the owner selected from North America, Europe, and the Orient. Today, sun-dappled paths lead visitors from one blossoming world to another.

WILD – FLOWER SOURCES

Applewood Seed Co.
833 Parfet St.
Lakewood, CO 80215
(seeds; free price list)

Clyde Robin Seed Co.
Box 2855
Castro Valley, CA 94546
(seeds; catalog $1.00)

Dutch Mountain Nursery
7984 N. 48th St. Rt. 1
Augusta, MI 49012
(free price list)

Forest Farm
990 Tetherow Road
Williams, OR 97544
(catalog 50¢)

Gardens of the Blue Ridge
P.O. Box 10
Pineola, NC 28662
(catalog $1.00)

Green Horizons
500 Thompson
Kerrville, TX 78028
(seeds; free price list)

Lounsberry Gardens
Box 135
Oakford, IL 62673
(plants; catalog 25¢)

Prairie Seed Source
P.O. Box 83
North Lake, WI 53064
(free price list)

Putney Nursery
Route 5
Putney, VT 05346
(plants; catalog free)

Order from nursery closest to home (so habitat and growing season are similar). If there are no nurseries near you, order from nurseries north or west of you.

How to Make a Butterfly Kite

Spring is in the air and nothing says it as well as a kite soaring overhead. To add to the thrill of these blustery days, try flying a kite that you've made yourself following these simple instructions.

SUPPLIES
—3 dowels (3/16″ diameter, 36″ long)
—flat board (3′ long, 8″ wide)
—about 25 nails and a hammer
—string (25 lb. test, at least 13′ long)
—paper (thin, strong, white wrapping paper or a 38″ x 24″ sheet)
—1 small brush (for spreading glue)
—white glue
—utility knife
—scissors
—spool of thread 1″ in diameter; rubber bands; 2 pencils
—broom straws (18 straws, each 6½″ long)
—thin cardboard (2 pieces, each 3″ x 6″)
—several colors of paint
—paint brush
—colored cloth or ribbon (cut into 20 strips, each 2′ long, ¾″ wide)

INSTRUCTIONS
Bending the Dowels
1. Put 2 dowels in bathtub; weight down; cover with hot water; leave overnight.
2. On the flat board, draw a curve with 20″ radius (tie pencil to a 22″ string; hold pencil at the rear center of the board; with other hand hold string 20″ away from board; now draw the curve). Drive a nail every 4″ along this curve. Bend dowels along the outside of the curve and hold in place with more nails. Let dowels dry 24 hours; remove.

Making the Frame
3. Cut notches 3/16″ from both ends of curved dowels.

4. Cut two 24″-long strings and tie an overhand knot at each end. Then tie a slip knot at each end. Place knots over ends of dowels so string rests in notches. Adjust knots so the ends of each bow are about 20½″ apart.
5. Lay one bow over the other (see pattern), forming an oval center section with its ends about 11″ apart. The angle of the bow strings to the horizontal base-line of the kite is 60 degrees.
6. Cut 3rd dowel into 2 pieces: one 15″ long; one 3½″.
7. Tightly lash the 15″ piece to points A and B. The dowel should extend 2″ beyond both ends of the oval center.
8. Tightly lash the 3½″ piece to points G, H, and I.
9. Check frame for symmetry; adjust.
10. Brush white glue over all the knots. Weight frame to keep it flat while drying.

Use nails to shape dowel as it dries.

Lash curved dowels together to make kite frame.

Attaching Body to Frame

15. Unfold the paper and center the kite frame on it. Starting at point A, bend tabs over the dowels and glue tabs to the paper. Paste 4 tabs on each side of A, then paste from B to E and B to F. Now finish pasting A to C and A to D.

16. Cut 2 strips of paper, 1″ wide and 20″ long, from the scraps. Glue them over the bow strings, from C to E and D to F.

17. Stiffen outer-curved portions of the wings by taping broom straws in place (see pattern).

18. For the butterfly head and tail, cut thin cardboard as shown in the drawing. Glue the square tab on the head to the kite frame. Glue the squared-off end of the tail to the frame.

19. Now paint the kite, copying the natural pattern of a butterfly.

Snip V-cuts to ease folding the tabs over the kite frame.

Making the Butterfly Body

11. Fold the 38″ x 24″ sheet of paper in half, so it is 19″ x 24″. Crease the fold, then open up paper.

12. Place frame on paper, so 15″ dowel lies in fold. Use a rubber band to attach a pencil to either side of spool of thread. The spool will act as a spacer to keep the pencils and the two lines they trace 1″ apart. Using this device, trace outline of kite onto paper. Then place a yardstick along the bow strings and draw one straight line from end to end of each bow.

13. Draw the upper and lower wing curves on the outer side of the bow string. The upper curve should be about 12″ long and 3½″ wide at its center. The lower, wavy curve is about 9½″ long and 3″ wide at its center (see pattern).

14. Lift frame off paper; refold paper. Hold edges together with paper clips placed about 6″ apart. Cut along the outer pencil lines. Then snip out V-cuts (cut to the inner pencil line) leaving tabs about 1″ wide for fastening the paper to the frame.

Bridling the Kite

20. To bridle the kite, cut a 38″ length of string. On the front of the kite (the frame is at the back), poke 2 small holes at A, 2 at B. At A, pass the string through one hole, around the lashing, and back through the other hole. Make a slip knot and tighten. Do the same at B. 14″ from upper knot, grab the string into a small loop and loosely knot it. The flying line will be attached to this loop.

Attaching the Tail

21. This kite has 2 tails. To attach them to the kite, cut two 10″ lengths of string. Using square knots, tie a loop in the middle of each string. Poke holes in the paper at E and F. Tie a loop to the frame at E and F by pushing the loose ends of the looped strings through the holes, wrapping them twice around the dowels, and tying them off with a square knot. Brush knots with glue.

22. Lay kite on floor and pick up by center of bridle. It should be absolutely horizontal level. If not, glue small pieces of paper to outer edges of the lighter side until kite is level.

23. Kite tails: Tie the ends of the 2′ long ribbons together, leaving an inch or so free to flare out. For an 8-knot wind, about a 20′ tail is needed (more wind, add more tail). Both tails must be same size and weight. Tie tails to loops made in step 21.

Tape stiff straws to outer part of wing to add strength.

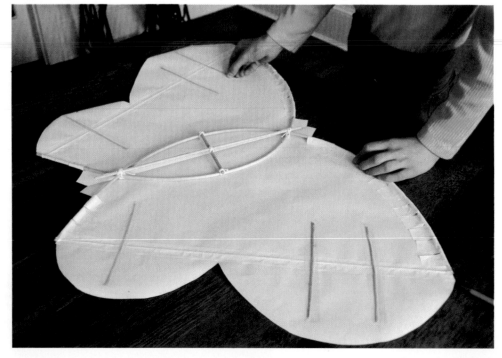

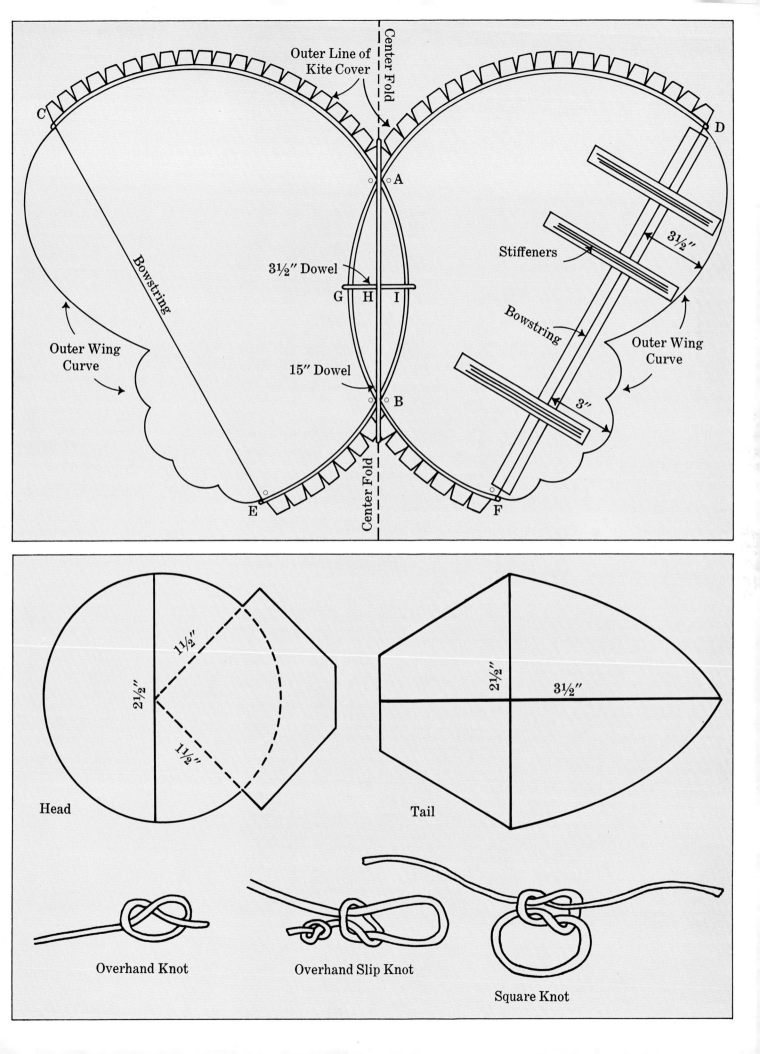

A young girl is overjoyed to find high tide has not destroyed the castle her family built on Rialto Beach in Olympic National Park.

Summer

Summer. To the castle builder sprinting down the sand, this season seems the normal order of things, the way nature ought to conduct herself the year round. Children can race outside without a coat, enjoy a swim without a cold. Trees look like trees instead of their own upended roots. Birds come into the yard without the goad of hunger or the lure of seeds and suet. Summertime—and the livin' is easy.

Summer is nature's cruising speed, a steady purr in high gear after the fitful shiftings and accelerations of spring. Wildlife's breeding boundaries so bitterly fought over begin to blur as parents proudly lead their young into wider worlds. No inchworm gauged the icicle's growth—but there he goes now, like a crazed concertina, quarter-inching across a leaf a grope at a time, too busy to wonder at the miracle just under his feet.

There the green plant builds cell upon cell, feeding on sunshine by a process we can label but not explain. By the simple sorcery of photosynthesis, green plants of field and forest feed creatures from inchworm to elk, with enough left over to make a growth investment in next summer's sprouts.

In its daily broad-jump across the horizons the summer sun hangs high and motionless, landing at last in a cloud of color, impatient to be up and leaping again. Days grow longer, nights grow shorter, and to that elemental drumbeat marches much of nature, for it is the length of light and darkness that bids the ragweed bloom and the migrant move on.

Summertime, and the lazin' is easy. But when holidays dawn, the celebrations are as big as all outdoors. Parades. Picnics. Fireworks. Family reunions. "Land sakes, Bobby, how you've grown!" Indeed the little fellow *has* grown. Kids sprout up twice as fast in spring as in fall. Then, after a gawky summer, they put on weight five times as fast in fall as they did in spring. No one knows why.

And no one cares. It's summer. "Bobby, be a good boy and pass the mustard."

85.

Fox.glove (*Digitalis purpurea*)
Trailing Rose (*Rosa arvensis*)

JUNE

June 24th. Midsummer Day.

The Cuckoo is beginning to change his tune, a little later he will be saying 'Cuc-cuckoo', instead of 'Cuckoo'. There is an old super-stition concerning the Cuckoo's cry in the South of England. If when you hear the Cuckoo, you begin to run and count the cuckoo's crys; and continue running until out of ear-shot, you will add as many years to your life as you count calls, — at least so the old women tell you in Devonshire. There are a good many rhymes about the Cuckoo:

In April Cuckoo sings his lay,
In May I sing all day,
In June I change my tune,
In July away I fly,
In August go I must.'

'The Cuckoo is a fine bird,
She whistles as she flies
And as she whistles, Cuckoo!
The bluer grow the skies.'

June 25th.

Went for a long country walk through Catherine de Barnes, Hampton in Arden, Bickenhill and Elmdon. Everywhere the lanes were fragrant with Wild Roses, and Honeysuckle, and the breeze came to us over the hedges laden with the perfume of the Clover-fields and grass meadows. The grasses of all kinds were lovely, all along the wayside. I found the Meadow Sweet in bloom in many places, Gathered Self-heal and Great Burnet among the meadow grass, and Dog-wood and the white, waxen blos-some of the 'Trailing Rose' from the hedges. We picniced under the hedge, with pink and white Clover bloom and tall grasses nodding round our heads, while a pair of excited Robins chattered and fluttered in the bushes round us, evidently very curious as to what we were about, down in their field-corner. Saw a great number of beautiful little Dragon-flies, — pale blue, with black markings, at a wayside pond, and Yellow Water-Lillies in full bloom on Elm-don Park pool!

June 28. Second day of continuous rain; Earth-quake shocks are recorded in this morning's papers, as having occurred yesterday in some of the Western counties of England and South Wales, extending from Bristol to the Mumbles.

June 30 Scarlet Poppy, Sow Thistle, Plume Thistle and Wild Migonette in flower.

June has been a very hot month with a large per centage of sun-shine and frequent thunder-storms.

The Glorious Fourth

Fireworks

They rise like sudden fiery flowers
　　That burst upon the night,
Then fall to earth in burning showers
　　Of crimson, blue, and white.

Like buds too wonderful to name,
　　Each miracle unfolds,
And catherine-wheels begin to flame
　　Like whirling marigolds.

Rockets and roman candles make
　　An orchard of the sky,
Whence magic trees their petals shake
　　Upon each gazing eye.

James Reeves

The Gift Outright

The land was ours before we were the land's.
She was our land more than a hundred years
Before we were her people. She was ours
In Massachusetts, in Virginia;
But we were England's, still colonials,
Possessing what we still were unpossessed by,
Possessed by what we now no more possessed.
Something we were withholding made us weak
Until we found out that it was ourselves
We were withholding from our land of living,
And forthwith found salvation in surrender.
Such as we were we gave ourselves outright
(The deed of gift was many deeds of war)
To the land vaguely realizing westward,
But still unstoried, artless, unenhanced,
Such as she was, such as she would become.

Robert Frost

America For Me

'Tis fine to see the Old World, and travel up and down
Among the famous palaces and cities of renown,
To admire the crumbly castles and statues of the kings,—
But now I think I've had enough of antiquated things.

So it's home again, and home again, America for me!
My heart is turning home again, and there I long to be
In the land of youth and freedom beyond the ocean bars,
Where the air is full of sunlight and the flag is full of
　　stars.

Oh, London is a man's town, there's power in the air;
And Paris is a woman's town, with flowers in her hair;
And it's sweet to dream in Venice, and it's great to study
　　Rome,
But when it comes to living, there is no place like home.

Oh, it's home again, and home again, America for me!
I want a ship that's westward bound to plough the
　　rolling sea,
To the blessed Land of Room Enough beyond the ocean
　　bars,
Where the air is full of sunlight and the flag is full of
　　stars.

Henry van Dyke

Innominatus

Breathes there a man with soul so dead,
Who never to himself hath said,
"This is my own, my native land!"
Whose heart hath ne'er within him burn'd
As home his footsteps he hath turn'd
From wandering on a foreign strand?
If such there breathe, go, mark him well;
For him no Minstrel raptures swell;
High though his titles, proud his name,
Boundless his wealth as wish can claim;
Despite those titles, power, and pelf,
The wretch, concentred all in self,
Living, shall forfeit fair renown,
And, doubly dying, shall go down
To the vile dust from whence he sprung,
Unwept, unhonour'd, and unsung.

Sir Walter Scott

Our National Bird

Bald eagles diligently care for their young eaglet from its birth in late winter or early spring until it begins to fly and hunt in 11 or 12 weeks. Their high-rise nest of sticks and grass is built near the top of a tall tree and added on to each year until it becomes gargantuan, weighing up to a ton or more. Some old nests are 8 feet across and 10 feet deep, dwarfing even the parents, who may stand 3 feet high, have a wingspread of 7 to 8 feet, and weigh up to 16 pounds. But, indomitable as the bald eagle seems to be, encroaching civilization and the use of DDT have seriously diminished its numbers in the contiguous United States. As recently as the early 1950s, there were many thousand pairs of bald eagles in the lower 48 states; now there are just over 1,000 pairs. Because its nesting and winter roosting trees are being destroyed by the building of roads, homes, and recreation areas along shorelines, and because it is still being shot, the great symbol of America struggles against unnatural odds to keep its breed alive.

Man's reverence for bald eagles dates back to earliest human history. Primitive man, staring into the skies, marveled at the giant birds whose mysterious powers let them soar to the limits of human vision and beyond. They sailed the skies with a sense of freedom that, in the minds of the ancients, bridged the chasm between the world of man and the land of spirits. For this reason, eagles were released during the funeral rites of ancient Egyptians to bear the souls of deceased rulers to the heavens. The legions of Rome, marching behind the eagle's image, were neither the first nor the last to draw upon the form and majesty of these great symbolic birds for their inspiration.

Respect for the sacred character of the eagle permeated the religious and social beliefs of the North American Indians. The Cheyenne brave killed the eagle for its feathers but did so only with strict attention to ancient ceremonial details, which included a formal apology to the spirit of the bird. The brave went into his lodge alone and through the long, dark night sang the sacred tribal chants reserved for the occasion. The following morning he selected the place for capturing the eagle, a place readily seen by the eagle in the sky. There he dug a hole in which to crouch and wait, but he dug with great care, working only when there were no eagles in sight. Then he gathered long grass to lay over the pit as a roof.

On the day of the capture the warrior would bathe, then cover his body with oils to mask the man odor. Before the first yellow light of dawn he slipped off silently to crouch hidden in the pit beneath the brown grass. Above him, he placed a dead rabbit or other fresh bait, lashed down securely to prevent the eagle from swooping in and carrying it away.

At last the eagle would circle the blue morning sky, then come steadily and swiftly closer on its widespread wings. It would settle on the meat, begin tearing at it, and become so driven by its hunger that it would not see the brown hands reaching slowly up through the grass below it. Then the eagle would be dragged struggling and flapping down into the pit. There, according to Cheyenne custom, it could be killed in only one manner, by strangulation with a noose. Having taken eagles with his bare hands, the brave could walk with great pride among his people.

The ancient respect for eagles is reflected in the symbolism of the American eagle. The image of the bald eagle is imprinted on United States currency, is seen on pillars at the entrances to public buildings, and is used to decorate the walls of homes, offices, and public gathering places. The eagle lends its name freely to fraternal orders, chemical industries, to building and loan companies, towns, rivers, ranches, and mountains. One might think that the choice of this king of wild birds as the national symbol was inevitable, but the eagle had its competitors and even its detractors.

At about two o'clock in the afternoon of July 4, 1776, the members of the Continental Congress signed the Declaration of Independence. They then discussed what they should do about an official seal, which would be the national coat of arms and would state to the world that this nation had formally declared itself an independent sovereign republic. The Congress assigned three of its most respected members to the task, men who had also played major roles in writing the Declaration: Benjamin Franklin, John Adams, and Thomas Jefferson.

The committee, after six weeks of agonizing debate, completed its report and submitted it to Congress. Congress, however, was unable to reach agreement, and the ill-fated report was tabled for four years, leaving the infant nation to manage as best it could without benefit of an official seal. In 1780 and again in 1782 new committees were appointed. At this point the only lasting result of six years of discussion was the motto *E pluribus unum*, credited to Thomas Jefferson. Finally, unable to agree on the proposals of any of them, Congress simply handed the project over to its secretary, Charles Thomson. It was he who made the eagle the central figure in his design, and insisted that it was to be an American bald eagle. In one talon the fierce looking bird carried an unlikely olive branch, in the other a bundle of arrows. Within a week it was adopted by Congress as the Great Seal of the United States.

It was not, however, universally approved. One leader unconvinced of its

merit was Benjamin Franklin, who, in a letter to his daughter in 1784, said, "I wish that the bald eagle had not been chosen as the representative of our country; . . . he does not get his living honestly; you may see him perched on some dead tree, where, too lazy to fish for himself, he watches the labor of the fishing-hawk; when that diligent bird has at length taken a fish, and is bearing it to his nest for the support of his mate and young ones, the bald eagle pursues him and takes it from him."

Inevitably, individual bald eagles have been remembered for their exploits. None, however, has gained more lasting fame than a fabled eagle from northern Wisconsin that went south during the Civil War. This eagle would not have gone to war at all had it not been for a Chippewa Indian named Sky Chief who one day in 1861 looked skyward and noted the broad form of an eagle nest in the top of a towering pine tree. Ignoring the angry protests of the circling adult birds, he began chopping on the base of the tree. As the tree came crashing to earth, the young lone occupant of the nest was tossed free to flutter weakly in the underbrush, where it was pounced upon by the elated Sky Chief.

The eaglet proved to be less than an ideal pet. It showed constant signs of a nasty disposition, most often expressed in an effort to clamp its two sets of needle-sharp talons into the arms or face of its captor. Understandably, Sky Chief changed his mind about wanting an eagle. But he was practical enough to resist the urge to wring the bird's neck: as an item of barter the bird might bring some reward for all that chopping.

In the village of Eagle River, Sky Chief, proudly carrying his eagle, struck a trade with Daniel McCann, whose best offer was a bushel of yellow corn. "And for this paltry sum," an admirer wrote in later years, "was the noble bird sold from freedom to captivity . . . from the moans of the pines to the crash of battle, from obscurity to fame." McCann himself did not yet know precisely what he would do with an unfriendly bird possessed of a 7-foot wingspread and a pair of feet capable of disfiguring a man. But he had invested a bushel of corn in the deal, so he carried the eagle off to

Chippewa Falls. There he sold it to the owner of a store for $2.50, plus repeated assurance that the merchant would find his "pet" a good home.

Meanwhile, farm lads were trooping in from round about to join up with the Eau Claire Badgers, and the patriotic merchant presented the unit with a genuine American eagle. In honor of the President the soldiers named the young eagle "Old Abe," and henceforth "Old Abe" rode atop a small square platform mounted on a pole at the head of his company with the color guard. Some reporters insisted that when people along the route of march applauded, the majestic eagle would spread his wings. Others made the questionable claim that on these occasions he picked up in his bill a small flag lying on his platform.

By the time Old Abe had been with the "Eagle Regiment" for several months, and his conditioning to military life was as complete as could be expected, he became, in addition to a noble symbol of his country's might, something of a damned nuisance. When free around the encampment he would amuse himself by slashing blue uniforms hung on the line to dry, upsetting soup pots, and generally causing trouble. But by the time he had served out his hitch he had become a hero credited with more acts of intelligence and bravery than strict attention to detail could support.

During the summer of 1864 Old Abe, veteran of Vicksburg, Corinth, and other noted encounters, came home to Wisconsin with full honors. The handsome bird was formally presented to the governor of Wisconsin and allowed quarters in the basement of the state capitol. He rose to the zenith of show business in 1876 when, with funds especially appropriated by the state legislature, he was sent to represent Wisconsin at the Philadelphia Exposition.

Old Abe was twenty years old when he died of suffocation during a brief but smoky fire in the basement of the capitol. He has not to this day been forgotten. After death the honor accorded him was unique among the military figures to have served Wisconsin. He was mounted and displayed prominently in the state capitol, a constant reminder of the past when times were better for eagles.

George Laycock

Exceptionally keen vision and superb flying skills make the bald eagle a great hunter. While soaring at 500 feet it can spot a fish swimming a mile away, swoop down at 100 miles per hour, seize it with powerful talons, and use the momentum of its dive to jerk its victim out of the water. Besides catching fish, bald eagles kill and eat waterfowl, turtles, and mammals. When not hunting, the majestic bird perches for hours, motionless, but ever watchful.

Hot days and a vacation visit to the family homestead on the Dakota Plains recently triggered a vivid recollection of the days of my childhood. I walked through the barns where I had jumped in the dusty hay-mows and fed the horses and milked the cows. I followed the path down to the creek and the swimming hole where I had dived into cool, green water. In the grainfields I watched the combines gobble up stalks of wheat and oats and barley, and with these sights came the memory of one of the rare delights of my childhood, the arrival of the threshing crew, now long displaced by modern machinery.

The ripening of the grain and the coming of the threshing crew occurred shortly after the Fourth of July, so for me that noisy holiday will always be associated with harvest days. The Fourth of July in the 1920s meant family picnics, bunting-draped band-stands, and patriotic declamations. The local chapters of the American Legion and the VFW went "over the top" again with the brave popping of blank cartridges and mighty blasts of the French "75," removed from the courthouse lawn for the day. The base-ball team played its rival, tender swains wooed their loved ones on carnival rides and in hidden places. The farm folk would pause, stretch their work-hardened muscles, and join their neighbors in brief sociability before turning to the next big event, the arrival of the great steam threshing rig.

The horse-drawn reapers would already have traversed the fields, their rotating arms gathering the kernel-laden stalks of grain to be cut by the chattering blades and bound into bundles which hardworking crewmen then built into shocks ranged in uneven roads across the stubble. The threshing rig would proceed from farm to farm, with the farmers and their hired help gathering to bring the bundled grain to the thresher and then to haul the separated grain to the granary for storage or to the elevator in town for sale.

Farmers accustomed to solitary labor would gather in cooperative effort in the threshing ring, anxious to get the harvesting done. Yet a holiday spirit seemed to prevail. There was a great deal of reminiscing and reviving of oft-told jokes and devising of new ones. Threshing time was in the nature of a social, a church supper, or a festival. The threshing ring was still an important part of harvest activities until the middle 1930s.

A farmer's standing in the community was mightily enhanced by his wife's reputation as a housekeeper and cook. And such a reputation could only be gained or lost at the tables set for the men who endured those long days of threshing, during which the sun and the steam boiler provoked great thirst and gargantuan appetites. The atmosphere in the farmhouse would assume an air of tense anticipation. Who had set the heaviest laden table last year? What were the judgments of the men as they tilted back their chairs, sated and happy?

As harvest preparations began, Aunt Ethel would come from the village to bake pies and enjoy her annual social visit, and Sister Sue would arrive, expecting a return of help when the threshers came to her house. A hired girl and a teen-age niece or two usually completed the platoon. All the food was cooked on a wood stove into which corncobs and kindling were fed in just the right amounts and at just the critical times. What magic was wrought in those country kitchens to have so much fine food ready for transfer to large platters and transport to trestle tables set up in the dining room, on the porch, and, often, in the yard beneath shady elms!

Potatoes and vegetables were prepared by the peck; pies and cakes, by the dozen. And always there were several kinds of meat: smoked ham boiled to juicy tenderness in the washboiler; rounds of beef roasted moist and brown; chicken fried crisp and golden. Hot loaves and biscuits tested the mettle of the cook. Fresh and preserved, sweet and tart, the relishes and pickles contributed a change of pace. And finally came the bubbling, fruit-filled pies and richly frosted cakes.

My memories of threshing time are prone to include little recall of the heat, which fell like a physical weight on work-bent shoulders, the wheat chaff that worked its way itchingly under one's shirt, and the cracking strain of muscles forking heavy bundles of grain onto wagons. They are, rather, rich and clear in recollecting the sound of laughing voices and the joys of the harvest table.

Earl Bihlmeyer

Thomas Hart Benton's 1939 "Threshing Wheat" captures the drama of the Midwest harvest rite as it had been performed since the turn of the century. Neighbors pooled manpower and horsepower to bring in the crop while the weather held. Pitchforked into the maw of the thresher, the bundled wheat became a stream of brown grain to feed the hungry and a golden mountain of straw that children waited to climb.

Threshing Time

Summer in the Catskills for a city child like me passed in a dream and a cloud of blueberries. There were blueberries everywhere, all summer. Blueberries were almost friendly and even we, sidewalk Girl Scouts, could feel knowledgeable, competent, and unthreatened when we went picking. Blackberries, on the other hand, which also fruited for most of our vacation, were downright unfriendly. The brambles scratched legs and tangled hair; the berries deposited stones under teeth braces. Nevertheless, we ate blackberries and complained. We also ate elderberries and complained—they are sour.

The principal occupation of many mornings was a trip to some patch of sandy scrubland. We ducked under wire fences with 8-quart aluminum pots on our heads, looking like a helmeted troop from Mars or stragglers from a medieval tournament.

Though there were more than enough blueberries for us, for the always unseen owners of the bushes, and for the swarms of birds, we picked with the dedication of those who feel this is their only chance. There was also much competition for the honor of First Pot-Filler.

Our mothers were ever alert to the dangers of perishing in the wilderness of hunger and thirst, so we carried jars of water, sandwiches, and unbelievably, fruit, to sustain us while we labored. We picked and ate, including a lot of berries—almost as much as went into the pots. Even my dog ate the berries on the ground and low branches. As pots became too heavy to wear—we slung them on belts around our necks—we would take the pots off, put them on the ground, and leave the dog to guard them. We continued to pick, checking each handful for stems, greenie loopers, and such, and throwing it into the pot. The dog felt that such watchdogging deserved a reward. There he sat, grazing right out of the pots. On the way home his teeth were as blue as ours.

Parents who want their children to know the oldfashioned joys of berry-picking will find cultivating blueberries a double pleasure. The bushes' display of pink-and-white flower clusters is beautiful in May and June. They belong to the heath family, *Ericaceae*, and the genus *Vaccinium*. There are a number of varieties, ranging in habit from upland and reasonably drought-resistant, to bog-dwellers. The plants are quite adaptable and their only hard-and-fast requirements seem to be an acid (pH 4.5-5.2), well-drained soil.

The high-bush varieties have been developed as cultivated plants, and each bush will live decades and produce fruit from its third or fourth year. Pruning encourages larger berries than those normally found on wild plants. Mulching cuts down on watering chores. Since the plants do well even when untended, they are perfect choices for the lazy gardener who will appreciate the bountiful yield of fruit. Blueberries need cross-pollination for good yield. Therefore, at least two and ideally four varieties should be set near each other. Since birds also appreciate the berries, it is a good idea to cover the bushes with 1-inch netting (supported by poles) as soon as the berries begin to color.

There was some good-natured argument back in my picking days concerning terminology. Is it blueberry or huckleberry? Thinking over our varied crop, some of what we gathered *was* huckleberry rather than blueberry. The two fruits—to a nonbotanist—do look alike. Blueberries are truly blue, they bloom earlier, they frequently have a whitish or cloudy "bloom" on the berries, and they have numerous, soft, red-brown seeds. Huckleberries have ten or so hard, nut-like seeds, a dark blue-to-black shiny fruit which is really a drupe—like a cherry with many pits. The leaves and young stems of huckleberry bushes have brown resinous spots that look like blight, or varnish drops. Huckleberries are also heath plants, *Ericaceae*, but their genus is *Gaylussacia*. Unlike blueberries, huckleberries are not cultivated commercially.

My mother's blueberry staples were pie, jam, and blintzes. The fresh ones I just ate out of hand. However, one can quickly develop a large blueberry repertoire. Berries are good in muffins, pancakes, coffeecakes, and cornbread, with no major recipe adjustments. Just add 1 cup blueberries to each 2 cups of flour along with the rest of the dry ingredients. Blueberries are fairly sweet by themselves and will enhance almost any dessert, but if wild berries are used, add ¼ cup sugar.

Blueberry Summer

Mama's Blueberry Pie

3 cups flour, sifted
½ teaspoon salt
2 teaspoons baking powder
grated zest of 1 orange and its juice
　(no more than ½ cup juice)
2 eggs
½ cup vegetable oil
8 cups blueberries, washed
2 cups sugar, plus 2 tablespoons
1¼ teaspoons cinnamon
½ cup tapioca, granular

Sift flour, salt, and baking powder together. Add orange zest and eggs. Mix well. Add oil and enough orange juice until dough mixes smooth. Roll out crust to fit the bottom of a 9-inch spring-form pan; roll remaining dough for a top crust and cut vent holes in it. Toss blueberries with 2 cups of the sugar, 1 teaspoon cinnamon, and the tapioca. Fill pie shell and cover with top crust. Brush crust with oil and sprinkle with the remaining sugar and cinnamon.
Bake in a preheated 350° oven for 1¼ hours or until well browned.

Blueberry Slump, or Grunt

If cooked covered on top of the stove, this pudding with biscuit topping is a Slump; if it is baked uncovered, it is a Grunt.
2 cups blueberries
½ cup sugar
1 cup water
1 cup flour
2 teaspoons baking powder
¼ teaspoon salt
2 tablespoons butter
⅓ cup milk

Wild or cultivated, blueberries are sweet enough to eat off the bush. They ripen unevenly, inviting pickers back.

In a large, heavy saucepan or a flame-proof casserole combine blueberries, sugar, and water. Cook over low heat until sugar has dissolved, then raise heat to medium and simmer 5 minutes. Set aside. To make the biscuit dough, mix the flour, baking powder, salt, butter, and milk together in a bowl. Drop the dough by spoonfuls onto the hot blueberry mixture. Cover and cook for 20 minutes over low heat, or leave uncovered and bake 20 minutes in a 400° oven. Serve warm, plain or with cream. Serves 4-6.

Blueberry Blintzes

1 cup flour
1 teaspoon salt
2 eggs
1 cup water
butter

To make batter, sift flour and salt together. Beat eggs and water together in another bowl and add gradually to flour mixture. Let stand for at least ½ hour. Heat a little butter in a small frying pan, wipe out excess with a paper towel (save towel), and pour in enough batter to film the bottom of the pan. Tilt pan to spread batter evenly. Cook over low heat until top is dry and bottom begins to brown. Turn out onto clean towel, cooked side up. Wipe pan with buttered paper towel again and repeat.
1½ pounds dry cottage or pot cheese
3 eggs
¼ cup sugar
1 cup blueberries
1 teaspoon cinnamon
¼ teaspoon salt
2 tablespoons breadcrumbs (optional)
butter
sour cream
sugar

To make filling, mix cottage or pot cheese with eggs, sugar, blueberries, cinnamon, and salt. The mixture should be dry, not runny. Add breadcrumbs if necessary. Place a spoonful of the filling in the center of each pancake and fold up, envelope-fashion. Fry in butter until golden brown and serve hot with sour cream and sprinkled with sugar. Makes 10 blintzes.
Barbara Charton

Why Presidents Fish

A solitary angler pulls in a bream as dawn tints the still waters of Georgia's Okefenokee Swamp.

That Presidents have taken to fishing seems to me worthy of investigation. I think I have discovered the reason: it is the silent sport. One of the few opportunities given a President for the refreshment of his soul and the clarification of his thoughts by solitude lies through fishing. As I have said in another place, it is generally realized and accepted that prayer is the most personal of all human relationships. Everyone knows that on such occasions men and women are entitled to be alone and undisturbed.

Next to prayer, fishing is the most personal relationship of man; and of more importance, everyone concedes that the fish will not bite in the presence of the public, including newspapermen.

Fishing seems to be one of the few avenues left to Presidents through which they may escape to their own thoughts, may live in their own imaginings, find relief from the pneumatic hammer of constant personal contacts, and refreshment of mind in rippling waters. Moreover, it is a constant reminder of the democracy of life, of humility and of human frailty. It is desirable that the President of the United States should be periodically reminded of this fundamental fact—that the forces of nature discriminate for no man.

Strong primary instincts—and they are useful instincts—get rejuvenation by a thrust into the simpler life. For instance, we do not catch fish in the presence of, or by the methods of, our vast complex of industrialism, nor in the luxury of summer hotels, nor through higher thought, for that matter. In our outdoor life we get repose from the troubles of soul that this vast complex of civilization imposes upon us in our working hours and our restless nights. Association with the placid ripples of the waves and the quiet chortle of the streams is soothing to our "het-up" anxieties.

I am for fishing for fun as a contribution to constructive joy because it gives an excuse and an impulse to take to the woods and to the water. Moreover, fishing has democratic values because the same privilege of joy is open to the country boy as to the city lad. (And equally to his properly brought up city or farmer dad.)

Our standards of material progress include the notion and the hope that we shall lessen the daily hours of labor on the farm, at the bench, and in the office. We also dream of longer annual holidays and more of them, as scientific discovery and mass production do our production job faster and faster. But they dull the souls of men. Even now, the great majority of us really work no more than eight hours a day. And if we sleep eight hours we have eight hours in which to ruminate and make merry or stir the caldron of evil. This civilization is not going to depend upon what we do when we work so much as what we do in our time off.

The moral and spiritual forces of our country do not lose ground in the hours we are busy on our jobs; their battle is the leisure time. We have great machinery for joy, some of it destructive, some of it synthetic, some of it mass production. We go to chain theatres and movies; we watch somebody else knock a ball over the fence or kick it over the goal post. I do that too and I believe in it. I do, however, insist that no organized joy has values comparable to the outdoors. . . . We gain none of the rejuvenating cheer that comes from return to the solemnity, the calm and inspiration of primitive nature.

Contemplation of the eternal flow of the stream, the stretch of forest and mountain, all reduce our egotism, soothe our troubles, and shame our wickedness. And in it we make a physical effort that no sitting on cushions, benches, or sidelines provides. To induce people to take this joy they need some stimulant from the hunt, the fish or the climb. I am for fish.

Now, if we want fish we have to reserve some place for them to live. They only occur in the water, but it happens that nature adapted them to clean water. I suppose that was because nature foresaw no fishing beatitudes along a sewer.

This question of pollution has a multitude of complications. There are as many opinions about pollution as there are minds concerning it. Pollution exists in different waters in different degrees; from ships, factories, coal mines, chemical works in cities and towns—to mention only a few of them. Many of these things damage public health, destroy the outdoor appeal of the streams, and all of them damage the fish.

There are two things I can say for sure: two months after you return from a fishing expedition you will begin again to think of the snowcap on the distant mountain peak, the glint of sunshine on the water, the excitement of the dark blue seas, and the glories of the forest. And then you buy more tackle and more clothes for next year. There is no cure for these infections.

And that big fish never shrinks.

Herbert Hoover

Journey Into Summer

America has many summers.
Its continental span embraces the summer of the shore,
the summer of the forest, the summer of the Great Plains, the summer
of the mountains. We had chosen
our general route to carry us through the greatest variety.
Thus on a golden day in June we set out together. Once more
we were adventuring across the months
of an American season. We were at the beginning of what
the old-time writers would have called "our joyful travels" through
the many summers of the land.

Edwin Way Teale

Rainbows of stone plunge from the rim to the floor of the Grand Canyon, etching a path for visitors through millions of years of geological history. Even before life began, the oldest rocks of these ancient walls were being formed. Layer by layer, the earth above them grew into a vast plateau, only to have the Colorado River slice down through it over the centuries, exposing those prehistoric rocks once again. Today, the Colorado roars through a mile-deep, 217-mile-long canyon, still excavating a deeper course through the earth's past.

But it is light and color that dramatize the spectacle of the Canyon. As the sun arcs daily across the sky, the angle of light changes from moment to moment, illuminating the landscape

with a kaleidoscope of variations.

Further west, vivid color creates a spectacle of another sort: a desert awash with a sea of poppies. In the Mojave Desert (left) survival depends on enduring or escaping the sun. Poppy seeds survive by lying dormant until a rare cloudburst prods them to bloom quickly and scatter their seed.

The stunted Monterey Cypresses along California's Seventeen-Mile Drive (opposite) make another kind of climatic adaptation. In this land of endless Indian Summer, gale-force winds sweep across craggy cliffs, sculpting the trees into contorted symbols of survival. Below, shimmering beaches and ocean beckon vacationers to make the Pacific one of their journeys into summer.

As summer begins to sizzle, cooler retreats beckon with the promise of relief. At the beaches or in the mountains, America's eastern vacationlands offer diversity and delight.

Misty and cool, Niagara Falls (at right) attracts honeymooners and urban refugees alike with its thundering wall of water. Visitors may walk behind the falls, helicopter over it, or go boating at its frothing base.

Farther east, along the coast, the glacially deposited hook of Cape Cod (top) offers both seashore and serene marsh. Here, in a quiet cove, gulls while away the summer waiting for each returning tide to bring the next course of tiny crabs.

Another well-known watering spot is Cape Hatteras National Seashore

(above), just off the coast of North Carolina. Like all barrier reefs, this 71-mile stretch of sand is dynamic: its seaward edge is constantly being nibbled away as the bayside grows in ever-widening marshes. Encroaching tides have claimed two previous light-houses, and waves have even lapped at the base of the present one.

The mountains of the east hold a quieter appeal. Along Virginia's Sky-line Drive (middle), motorists can meander for 96 miles atop the crest of the Blue Ridge and share a scenic picnic spot with backpackers on the Appalachian Trail. In New Hamp-shire's White Mountains, hikers have set their compasses for centuries by a storied landmark, the Old Man of the Mountains (left).

The refined, simple beauties of the East had not prepared early explorers for the grandiose marvels that waited on the other side of the Great Plains. At the first recorded sighting of Old Faithful, one member of the party wrote, "We had within a distance of 50 miles seen what we believed to be the greatest wonders of the continent." The group reportedly sat transfixed through nine consecutive eruptions. Old Faithful is still a dazzling performer, averaging 22 outpourings a day.

East of Yellowstone soars a fountain of stone. Devil's Tower (opposite), a rendezvous of the Old West, is a fluted upthrust of igneous rock that beckons to travelers across Wyoming's high and lonesome land.

The deserts of the Southwest stretch into eight states. To Lt. Joseph Ives, a government explorer, the colorful shales, marls, and sandstones of northeast Arizona seemed to be painted upon the landscape. Hence his name for it, Painted Desert (above). Millions of years before the discovery of Monument Valley (above, left), it was a high plateau. Today, the remaining mesas and buttes bear silent testimony to the erosive force of wind and weather.

One of the last reaches of the country to be mapped was a lush rain forest on the western slopes of the Olympic Mountains. Now part of Olympic National Park, its moss-hung trails offer one of the continent's most exotic summer adventures.

Life at the Edge of the Sea

The edge of the sea is a strange and beautiful place. All through the long history of Earth it has been an area of unrest where waves have broken heavily against the land, where the tides have pressed forward over the continents, receded, and then returned. For no two successive days is the shore line precisely the same. Not only do the tides advance and retreat in their eternal rhythms, but the level of the sea itself is never at rest. It rises or falls as the glaciers melt or grow, as the floor of the deep ocean basins shifts under its increasing load of sediments, or as the earth's crust along the continental margins warps up or down in adjustment to strain and tension. Today a little more land may belong to the sea, tomorrow a little less. Always the edge of the sea remains an elusive and indefinable boundary.

The shore has a dual nature, changing with the swing of the tides, belonging now to the land, now to the sea. On the ebb tide it knows the harsh extremes of the land world, being exposed to heat and cold, to wind, to rain and drying sun. On the flood tide it is a water world, returning briefly to the relative stability of the open sea.

Only the most hardy and adaptable can survive in a region so mutable, yet the area between the tide lines is crowded with plants and animals. In this difficult world of the shore, life displays its enormous toughness and vitality by occupying almost every conceivable niche. Visibly, it carpets the intertidal rocks; or half hidden, it descends into fissures and crevices, or hides under boulders or lurks in the wet gloom of sea caves. Invisibly, where the casual observer would say there is no life, it lies deep in the sand, in burrows and tubes and passageways. It tunnels into solid rock and bores into peat and clay. It encrusts weeds or drifting spars or the hard, chitinous shell of a lobster. It exists minutely, as the film of bacteria that spreads over a rock surface or a wharf piling; as spheres of protozoa, small as pinpricks, sparkling at the surface of the sea; and as Lilliputian beings swimming through dark pools that lie between the grains of sand.

The shore is an ancient world, for as long as there has been an earth and sea there has been this place of the meeting of land and water. Yet it is a world that keeps alive the sense of continuing creation and of the relentless drive of life. Each time that I enter it, I gain some new awareness of its beauty and its deeper meanings, sensing that intricate fabric of life by which one creature is linked with another, and each with its surroundings.

There is a common thread that links these scenes and memories—the spectacle of life in all its varied manifestations as it has appeared, evolved, and sometimes died out. Underlying the beauty of the spectacle there is meaning and significance. It is the elusiveness of that meaning that haunts us, that sends us again and again into the natural world where the key to the riddle is hidden.

Rachel Carson

Along Pacific shores, calm pools alternate with crashing waves up to 40 feet high. Humans could not survive such poundings, but seashore animals have evolved ways to cope. Discs on the undersides of sea stars and sea anemones, for example, solidly anchor them to both sand and rocks while the life-sustaining water rushes over them.

Ark Shell

Heart Cockle

Banded Tulip Shell

Shark Eye Moon Snail

Serrated Pen Shell

Atlantic Bay Scallop

Fig Shell

Kitten Paws

Left-Handed Whelk

If you told people you collected skeletons, they would look at you oddly and consider you a very strange sort of person. But if you told them you collected shells—that would be an entirely different matter! Actually, shells are the skeletons of the animals that live inside them.

These animals are called mollusks. Snails are called univalves. When you see "uni" at the start of a word, it means "one" and univalves have one shell. Bivalves, such as clams, oysters, and scallops, have two shells. "Bi" means "two" as in the word "bicycle."

There are lots and lots of both univalves and bivalves to be found on our beaches. People have collected and admired them for centuries.

Did you know that Indians in all parts of the world including the United States used shells as money? Today thousands of people prowl the beaches collecting shells as a hobby.

One of the best places in the world for shell collecting is Sanibel Island, off the west coast of Florida. It has miles of clean beaches. The sea bottom has a healthy and thriving animal community, and a three-day nor'wester may toss millions of tons of fresh shells onto its beaches.

Even before sunrise eager collectors walk along the water's edge, trying to get first pick of the sea's latest offerings. There are always a lot from which to choose including shark eyes, kitten paws, fig shells, pen shells, tulips, olives, conchs of several kinds, king's crowns, cockles, sunset tellins and dozens of others.

Some people make shells their life's work and sell them in roadside shops or by mail. Some trade with other collectors all over the world. A person can assemble a hundred or more different types without much trouble. They are often displayed in a glass-topped table, sewn onto hats or dresses, or made into jewelry: earrings, cufflinks and tie clasps. Some talented artists have made shell pictures that are truly beautiful. The artist may find only a few dozen shells in every thousand that are suitable for his particular work of art.

One thing is certain: Shells are fun—fun to collect, to trade with friends, to use as decorations or fun to make into other things. There are a few thousand kinds in the seas and on the beaches—just waiting for you to start your collection.

Russ Kinne

Hunting Treasure on the Beach

Seashore explorers search in shallow pools and clumps of wet seaweed for perfect shells. Low tide is the luckiest time to hunt because the outgoing water uncovers shells that have recently been washed up from the ocean floor and have not yet been broken. Incoming tides litter America's beaches with about 6,000 kinds of seashells, a lifetime challenge to collectors.

Jody and the Flutter-Mill

Jody stood a minute, balancing the hoe on his shoulder. The clearing itself was pleasant if the unweeded rows of young shafts of corn were not before him. The wild bees had found the chinaberry tree by the front gate. They burrowed into the fragile clusters of lavender bloom as greedily as though there were no other flowers in the scrub. It occurred to him that he might follow the swift line of flight of the black and gold bodies, and so find a bee-tree, full of amber honey.

He stood his hoe against the split-rail fence. He walked down the cornfield until he was out of sight of the cabin. He cut into the sand road and began to run east. It was two miles to the Glen, but it seemed to Jody that he could run forever. There was no ache in his legs, as when he hoed the corn. He slowed down to make the road last longer. Where he walked now, the scrub had closed in, walling in the road with dense sand pines. The sky was framed by the tawny sand and the pines. Small clouds were stationary, like bolls of cotton. As he watched, the sunlight left the sky a moment and the clouds were gray.

"There'll come a little old drizzly rain before nightfall," he thought.

The down grade tempted him to a lope. The tar-flower was in bloom, and fetter-bush and sparkleberry. He slowed to a walk, so that he might pass the changing vegetation tree by tree, bush by bush, each one unique and familiar. He reached the magnolia tree where he had carved the wildcat's face. The growth was a sign that there was water nearby. It seemed a strange thing to him, when earth was earth and rain was rain, that scrawny pines should grow in the scrub, while by every branch and lake and river there grew magnolias. Dogs were the same everywhere, and oxen and mules and horses. But trees were different in different places.

"Reckon it's because they can't move none," he decided. They took what food was in the soil under them.

The road dropped below him twenty feet to a spring. The bank was dense with magnolia and loblolly bay, sweet gum and gray-barked ash. He went down to the spring in the cool darkness of their shadows. A sharp pleasure came over him. This was a secret and lovely place.

A spring as clear as well water bubbled up from nowhere in the sand. It was as though the banks cupped green leafy hands to hold it. There was a whirlpool where the water rose from the earth. Beyond the bank, the parent spring bubbled up at a higher level, cut itself a channel through white limestone and began to run rapidly down-hill to make a creek. The creek joined Lake George, Lake George was a part of the St. John's River, the great river flowed northward and into the sea. It excited Jody to watch the beginning of the ocean. There were other beginnings, true, but this one was his own. He liked to think that no one came here but himself and the wild animals and the thirsty birds.

He was warm from his jaunt. He rolled up the hems of his blue denim breeches and stepped with bare dirty feet into the shallow spring. His toes sank into the sand. It oozed softly between them and over his bony ankles. The water was so cold that for a moment it burned his skin. Then it made a rippling sound, flowing past his pipe-stem legs, and was entirely delicious. He walked up and down, digging his big toe experimentally under smooth rocks he encountered. A school of minnows flashed ahead of him down the growing branch. He chased them through the shallows. They were suddenly out of sight as though they had never existed. He crouched under a bared and overhanging live-oak root where a pool was deep, thinking they might

reappear, but only a spring frog wriggled from under the mud, stared at him, and dove under the tree root in spasmodic terror. He laughed.

"I ain't no 'coon. I'd not ketch you," he called after it.

He waded across to the opposite bank where the growth was more open. A low palmetto brushed him. It reminded him that his knife was snug in his pocket; that he had planned as long ago as Christmas to make himself a flutter-mill.

He had never built one alone. Grandma Hutto's son Oliver had always made one for him whenever he was home from sea. He went to work intently, frowning as he tried to recall the exact angle necessary to make the mill-wheel turn smoothly. He cut two forked twigs and trimmed them into two Y's of the same size. Oliver had been very particular to have the cross-bar round and smooth, he remembered. A wild cherry grew half-way up the bank. He climbed it and cut a twig as even as a polished pencil. He selected a palm frond and cut two strips of the tough fiber, an inch wide and four inches long. He cut a slit lengthwise in the center of each of them, wide enough to insert the cherry twig. He adjusted them carefully. He separated the Y-shaped twigs by nearly the length of the cherry cross-bar and pushed them deep into the sand of the branch bed a few yards below the spring.

The water was only a few inches deep but it ran strongly, with a firm current. The palm-frond mill-wheel must just brush the water's surface. He experimented with depth until he was satisfied, then laid the cherry bar between the twigs. It hung motionless. He twisted it a moment, anxiously, helping it to fit itself into its forked grooves. The bar began to rotate. The current caught the flexible tip of one bit of palm frond. The small leafy paddles swung over and over, up and down. It turned with the easy rhythm of the great watermill at Lynne that ground corn into meal.

Jody threw himself on the weedy sand and abandoned himself to the magic of motion. Up, over, down, up—the flutter-mill was enchanting.

A shaft of sunlight, warm and thin like a light patchwork quilt, lay across his body. He sank into the softness. The sky closed over him. He slept.

When he awakened, he thought he might still be dreaming. The sun was gone, and all the light and shadow. There were no black boles of live oaks, no glossy green of magnolia leaves, no pattern of gold lace where the sun had sifted through the branches. The world was all a gentle gray, and he lay in a mist as fine as spray from a waterfall.

As he left his nest, he stopped short. A deer had come to the spring while he was sleeping. The fresh tracks came down the east bank and stopped at the water's edge. They were sharp and pointed, the tracks of a doe. They sank deeply into the sand, so that he knew the doe was an old one and a large. Perhaps she was heavy with fawn. She had come down and drunk deeply from the spring not seeing him where he slept. Then she had scented him. There was a scuffled confusion in the sand where she had wheeled in fright. The tracks up the opposite bank had long harried streaks behind them. Perhaps she had not drunk, after all, before she scented him, and turned and ran with that swift, sand-throwing flight. He hoped she was not now thirsty, wide-eyed in the scrub.

He looked about for other tracks. The squirrels had raced up and down the banks, but they were bold, always. A raccoon had been that way, with his feet like sharp-nailed hands, but he could not be sure how recently. Only his father could tell for certain the hour when any wild things had passed by. Only the doe had surely come and had been frightened. He turned back again to the flutter-mill. It was turning as steadily as though it had always been there.

Jody looked at the sky. He could not tell the time of day in the grayness, nor how long he may have slept. He turned and galloped toward home. He heard the chickens clucking and quarreling and knew they had just been fed. He turned into the clearing. The weathered gray of the split-rail fence was luminous in the rich light. Smoke curled thickly from the stick-and-clay chimney. Supper would be ready on the hearth and hot bread baking in the Dutch oven. He hoped his father had not returned from Grahamsville. It came to him for the first time that perhaps he should not have left the place while his father was away. If his mother needed wood, she would be angry. Even his father would shake his head and say, "Son—". He heard old Caesar snort and knew his father was ahead of him.

The clearing was in a pleasant clatter. The horse whinnied at the gate, the calf bleated in its stall and the milch cow answered, the chickens scratched and cackled and the dogs barked with the coming of food and evening. He swung open the front paling gate and went to find his father.

Penny Baxter was at the wood-pile. Jody saw his father's big hands, big for the rest of him, close around a bundle of wood. He was doing Jody's work, and in his good coat. Jody ran to him.

"I'll git it, Pa."

He hoped his willingness, now, would cover his delinquency. His father straightened his back.

"I near about give you out, son," he said.

"I went to the Glen."

"Hit were a mighty purty day to go," Penny said. "Or to go anywhere. How come you to take out such a fur piece?"

It was as hard to remember why he had gone as though it had been a year ago. He had to think back to the moment when he had laid down his hoe.

"Oh." He had it now. "I aimed to foller the honey-bees and find a bee-tree."

"You find it?"

Jody stared blankly.

"Dogged if I ain't forgot 'til now to look for it."

He felt as foolish as a bird-dog caught chasing field mice. He looked at his father sheepishly. His father's pale blue eyes were twinkling.

"Tell the truth, Jody," he said, "and shame the devil. Wa'n't the bee-tree a fine excuse to go a-ramblin'?"

Jody grinned.

"The notion takened me," he admitted, "afore I studied on the bee-tree."

"That's what I figgered. How come me to know, was when I was drivin' along to Grahamsville, I said to myself, 'There's Jody now, and the hoein' ain't goin' to take him too long. What would I do this fine day, was I a boy?' And then I thought, 'I'd go a-ramblin'!'"

A warmth filled the boy that was not the low golden sun. He nodded.

"That's the way I figgered," he said.

"But your Ma, now," Penny jerked his head toward the house, "don't hold with ramblin'. Most womenfolks cain't see for their lives, how a man loves to ramble. I never let on you wasn't here. She said, 'Where's Jody?' and I said, 'Oh, I reckon he's around some'eres.'"

He winked one eye and Jody winked back.

"Men-folks has got to stick together in the name o' peace. You carry your Ma a good bait o' wood now."

Jody filled his arms and hurried to the house.

Marjorie Kinnan Rawlings

Summer Symphony

Have you listened to the chirping and clicking of insects on a warm summer evening? Did you know that you were listening to music? Not just noises, but songs with a beat and a message. You were hearing songs of love, war chants, and music made by a family chorus.

Crickets, katydids, cicadas, grasshoppers, and many other kinds of insects make music. The music has meaning, but only members of the same insect species can understand each song. These insects are called the singing insects, because the sounds they make have rhythm and melody. The rhythm is strong and clear. The melody is less easy to hear, but it is there in very high-pitched chirps.

Of course, insects don't really sing the way you do. When you sing, you force air from your lungs past your vocal cords. But most insects make sounds by using parts of their bodies as if they were playing musical instruments.

Crickets *fiddle* their songs much as a violinist uses a bow. The insect lifts its wings, then rubs one wing against the rough edge of the other wing. This makes a clicking sound the same way as when you run a piece of wood along a picket fence. The cricket rubs its wings together so quickly you can't hear the individual clicks. The cricket's name is supposed to sound like its song, *crick-et, crick-et.*

The cricket has many songs. One is a courtship song which the male sings to attract a female. When a female cricket hears it, she hops along the ground toward the sound looking for the male. How does she hear him? With "eardrums" on her knees! When she finds the male, he begins a new song for her. Then they mate.

Among most singing insects, only the males sing and the females are forever silent, but the female mole cricket does sing a soft reply to the male.

Since crickets are cold-blooded, their body functions speed up as the air temperature rises. By listening very carefully to the songs of a cricket, you can actually figure out how hot it is. The best cricket for this is the pale green snowy tree cricket, which lives in most parts of the United States. Count the number of times it chirps in 14 seconds, then add 40. The total will give you the temperature in degrees Fahrenheit.

Another singing insect is the katydid, which seems to tattle *Katy did, Katy didn't, Katy did.* True katydids sing only at night, and then often in unison. They do not miss a beat. When one begins its song, others join in. Katydids recognize each other by the melody of their songs. They make music by scraping their forewings back and forth together like the crickets. The edge of one wing has a blade-like scraper and the other has a row of teeth like a file. When they rub them together, the wings vibrate rapidly to make the song.

Most grasshoppers make scraping noises by rubbing their hind legs over a vein on their wings. Grasshoppers know what they are singing about, but their song is a mystery to us humans.

The cicada is a drummer, not a fiddler. It has the fanciest music-making instrument of all! The male has cavities like small drums in its body. The skin stretches across these cavities. The cicada makes its sound by moving a muscle to make the drumskins vibrate. The cicada's song doesn't sound like a drum, though. It sounds more like a rattling buzz.

What a racket a group of cicadas can make! In the forested areas of some southern states the insects have been so noisy near classrooms that school has had to be canceled!

One of the cicada's songs is a fight song. When another male cicada comes too near, his song seems to say, *If you come any closer you will have to fight!*

By recording different insect sounds, scientists are learning more about the meanings of the songs. They play back the tapes where the insects are and watch what the insects do when they hear their own songs or the songs of other insects.

By knowing the meanings of insect songs, scientists can fight insect pests. The beet leafhopper, a relative of the cicada, is a singing insect that eats the leaves of beets, tomatoes and other crops. Each year this insect damages ten million dollars' worth of crops. Scientists record the mating song of the beet leafhopper. Then they play the recording back in a field where the leafhoppers live and traps have been set. The sound lures the females away from the crops and into the traps. Without the females, the leafhoppers can't reproduce and the number of leafhoppers drops.

Perhaps soon humans will use the songs of other harmful insects to control them, without the need for poisons.

Patricia W. Spencer

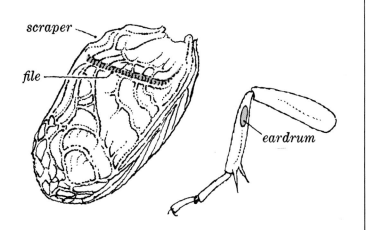

Male crickets rub together the scraper and file on their wings to sing. Their audience listens with ear "drums" located on their front legs.

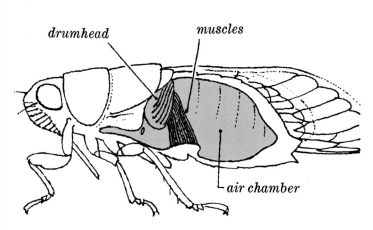

The cicada uses its "drum" to sing, not hear. Its muscles snap the drumhead over 200 times a second, making the air in the chamber vibrate.

Nature's Night-light

Like 10,000 candles, male Malaysian fireflies (top, right) light up a tree at night in the jungle. They all flash the light in their tails (above) at the same time so female fireflies can find them. They flash two times in one second, but the flashes look like only one to people watching. When a female finds a male, they mate. The fireflies that live in North America (right) also find mates by flashing their lights. Instead of sitting in a tree, males fly alone back and forth over the ground, flashing signals to females waiting in the grass.

Almost every boy and girl has seen fireflies blinking their lights on and off as they fly through the night. But did you know the firefly is actually sending a secret message when it flashes its light? It is a code that only certain other fireflies can understand.

Most of the fireflies you see at night are males. "Lady" fireflies seldom fly. Some kinds do not even have wings. In fact fireflies are not flies at all! They are soft-bodied beetles of the family *Lampyridae*.

When darkness comes the female fireflies crawl from deep in the grass or leaves where they have slept all day. They climb to the top of a blade of grass or onto the tip of a leaf where their light can be seen easily. Then they wait.

When the male fireflies awake each evening, they crawl to the tip of a leaf and fly off into the soft night air. They have two pairs of wings. The first pair is not used for flying at all; they are really two hard covers which protect the second pair of wings, the ones used for flying. These flying wings are very thin and easily broken. As the males fly, their bodies appear almost straight up and down, because they are suspended in the air from these wings. The end of their tail, where the light is, hangs down like a bright lantern in the night. At times the firefly may hold one pair of his three pairs of legs out from his body for balance.

Do all the fireflies you see on a summer night seem to look the same? Biologists have found more than 100 different kinds in the United States—almost every state has a few kinds. Each kind has its own flash signal! Only with these "family" codes do they find their own kind in the darkness.

Some fireflies blink quickly several times. Others blink a short signal, then leave their lights off for a long time before blinking again. One kind of firefly which lives in the eastern United States takes a "roller coaster" ride in the air while his light is on. He traces a "J" in the darkness with each blink. Fireflies blink more on warm, moist nights when the moon is not out. Fireflies are cold-blooded. The warm nights make their flashing machines blink faster, usually from June through August.

One scientist was able to fool some male fireflies. Every night he lay in the grass and blinked a tiny flashlight at the flying fireflies. After three weeks he learned their signals and was able to get fireflies to land on his flashlight. He found that the secret of the signals was to wait just the right length of time before flashing back at the firefly in the air. When a firefly flashed a "J" signal between six and ten feet away from him, he got ready. He held the flashlight close to the ground so its lens pointed down. When the firefly flashed again, the scientist counted two seconds (by saying one-thousand-one, one-thousand-two) and then blinked his flashlight on for one-half second. Each time he blinked, he lowered the flashlight, until finally the lens actually touched the ground. That made the firefly land near it.

Female fireflies waiting on the ground know which flashes in the air come from males of their own kind. The female flashes only after she has seen the right signal in the air. When the flying male sees the answering flash on the ground, he flies toward it and lands. His large compound eyes, which are actually hundreds of little eyes put together, help him to find the one on the ground. She will be his mate.

When the female firefly is ready to lay her eggs, she puts them into a tiny crack in the ground. Just imagine—the firefly eggs themselves glow in the dark! In about three weeks the eggs hatch into caterpillar-like larvae. The firefly larvae have two spots on their tails which glow. Sometimes on a spring night you can see these little dots of light when the larvae crawl in the grass. They eat snails and worms which they paralyze with their bite.

The larvae spend one or two summers underground. Then they build a small mud "igloo" and crawl inside to go to sleep. In about ten days the larvae have changed into grown-up fireflies. The adult firefly never eats, and lives only a few days. But every night of its life you can be sure it will be busy blinking secret messages with its light.

The light of the firefly is different from most other lights you are likely to see. It actually comes from a chemical reaction in its body. The glowing material is called "luciferin." It is cold light. Campfires and light bulbs, as you know, make heat when they make light. When the firefly makes light, there is no heat at all. You can let one blink on your finger without fear of being burned. Man still has to learn some of the secrets of how the firefly makes cold light, but that's another story.

Alan Linn

Autumn

As the trees of autumn carouse in harlequin costume, we take to cars and bikes and hiking shoes and picture windows for a better look. The colors were there all the time, but now we can see them as the frostbitten chlorophyll breaks down and drains its green away. Now we can see the birds' nests too, as autumn declassifies the top secrets of spring. And a scrubbed kid trudging back to a scrubbed classroom glances up and sees a river of birds undulating across the sky, bearing away the tiny mites born in the birdhouse he made in school last March. Autumn already? Where did the summer go?

As if unnerved by a chill north wind, the sun has headed south, taking with it the sweltering days, the long evenings of lingering daylight, the grumbling thunderstorms like stern grandmothers dragging skirts of rain across the land. Now the nights grow longer as they reclaim both ends of the day. Now the valleys turn misty, chilly, spooky in the moonlight as skeletal trees clutch at the scurrying hobgoblins of Hallowe'en.

The sun has been inching south since summer began, but only now do man and nature seem to notice. Goodbye to gardens whose naked stalks shrivel as their plump offspring come a-steaming to Thanksgiving tables. Goodbye to summer loves who may write yearning letters by autumn firesides—or find new romance at county fairs and hayrides. Goodbye to bare feet and bubble gum; not even autumn's apples can bribe teachers to tolerate either.

Yet, for many, this is the best of seasons. The larders of man and animals bulge with the rewards of summer's labor. Crisp mornings quicken the stride of hiker and hunter while homebodies bask in the warmth of fireglow. The fallen leaves bid us all pass quietly lest we disturb their sleep. And for every slumbering leaf, there is a bud.

149.

October

'Now Autumn's fire burns slowly along the woods,
And day by day the dead leaves fall and melt,
And night by night the monitory blast
Wails in the key-hole, telling how it pass'd
O'er empty fields, or upland solitudes,
Or grim, wide wave, and now the power is felt
Of melancholy, tenderer in it's moods,
Than any joy indulgent Summer dealt.'

William Allingham.

'O all wide places, far from feverous towns!
Great shining seas! pine-forests! mountains wild!
Rock-bosomed shores! Rough heaths, and sheep-cropt
downs!
Vast pallid clouds! blue spaces undefiled!
Room! give me room! give loneliness and air!
Free things and plenteous in your regions fair.

O God of mountains, stars and boundless spaces!
O God of freedom and of joyous hearts!
When thy face looketh forth from all men's faces;
There will be room enough in crowded marts:
Brood thou around me, and the noise is o'er;
Thy universe my closet with shut door.'

George Macdonald.

Migration

Moving to a solar drumbeat, many of the organisms of the earth are gripped in endless comings and goings that we call migrations. Yet the ways of migrants remain wreathed in mysteries. Not all life forms migrate; both squirrel and oak stay put and prosper year round. Dwellers in the Southern Hemisphere are less inclined to travel than are their northern neighbors. The stay-at-homes—among them man, whose feet follow his own whim and not the sun's—may well ask the migrants what makes them do it. What tells them to leave? What guides them on the journey? What calls them back? And why not simply stay home and save themselves the trouble?

Men have puzzled over these questions for thousands of years. But only in the last few decades scientists have begun to poke into some of the migrants' deeper secrets—and to pry loose some of the answers.

The tracks of the migrants lead in many directions. The earthworm migrates vertically, burrowing deeper into earth's warmth for the winter, tunneling up again in spring—a 15-inch trip, perfectly timed to meet the hungry robin that has just flown 1,500 miles from the south.

Lemmings troop across northern landscapes in impressive numbers, usually in spring and again in fall. A suicide march to compensate for overpopulation? Perhaps; more likely, the small rodents are simply moving from a depleted larder in search of a full one.

At the other end of the scale of tundra mammals are the large migrants. As the brief arctic summer draws near, caribou begin a trek that may end some 300 miles away. Pregnant cows hurry ahead of the herd to sheltered slopes where they can drop their calves. Then mothers and young struggle on to rejoin the herd and fatten in the greening lowlands. Far more dramatic are the famed migrations of grazers and browsers across the face of Africa. Zebra, wildebeest, gazelle, animals in the hundreds of thousands cloud the Serengeti in the early months of the year. When May heralds the dry season, the vast army dwindles, smaller herds break away in search of permanent grass near Lake Victoria or better browse in the bush country of Kenya. In eight months the scattered thousands begin to coalesce again, and the drama repeats.

Beneath the ocean, the tides of migration ebb and flow. Among the smallest of the migrants are the plankton of both salt water and fresh. Many of these creatures migrate toward the surface at night and sink deeper during the day. Some freshwater plankton may migrate from near the surface to a depth of 30 feet in a day; saltwater varieties may descend to 150 feet—no mean trek for a creature barely visible to the human eye.

Feeding on these smallest of travelers are the largest migrants of all, the whales. Most baleen species quit the polar seas—a rich broth of plankton—to bear their calves in warmer waters along the temperate shorelines.

The migrations of insects can be very beautiful—and terrifying. Huge swarms of locusts scourge Africa without warning, blotting out the sun, denuding croplands, clogging air intakes of spray planes, defying insecticides by sheer force of numbers.

Dragonflies migrate over considerable distances, and so do butterflies. Monarch butterflies wing hundreds of miles between Canada and wintering grounds in Mexico and California. And each new generation finds its ancestral wintering ground—even the same trees—in that tiny area without ever having been there before. The saga of migration offers few chapters more astounding than theirs.

One migrant seems to be reading the map upside-down: The pinkish Ross' gull leaves its Siberian nesting grounds and wings *northward* each autumn to the forbidding deep-freeze of the polar ice pack. But that's where the fry and plankton are; through the winter the gull dips its dinner from patches of open water in the ice-choked seas until the need to nest calls it southward each spring.

The birds are, of course, the most wondrous of the wanderers. Hundreds of species, billions of birds, sweep across vast stretches of land and sea. Harbingers of both spring and autumn, they pool in nervous flocks that flood into undulating rivers of birds, coursing toward the shrinking sunlands through time-worn canyons of air.

So it's not surprising that the world's champion commuter is a bird. The arctic tern summers in the far north, raising its chicks in crude nests scraped out of the tundra. Then it flies, almost literally, from pole to pole for a second summer in the Antarctic—a stupendous annual round-trip of as much as 22,000 miles.

In such amazing journeys, how do birds navigate? There seems to be no single answer. Some may follow landmarks below; flocks of kingbirds seem to use the Mississippi River as an interstate highway, banking this way and that as the river turns. Other flocks follow mountain ranges, often skirting shorelines rather than striking out across a body of open water.

But many species cross long stretches of featureless ocean. Some fly by night. Radar operators have spotted flocks sandwiched between cloud layers where they could see neither the sky above nor the landmarks below. Without visual cues, these navigators must depend on other guidance systems. But which ones?

Migrating Canada geese extend their long day's journey into the night, rushing south over the Adirondacks on their way to East Coast wintering grounds.

Sockeye salmon, following subtle wafts of extremely diluted perfume sent to the ocean by stream-side plants, migrate to the same spawning ground where they were born. Monarch butterflies on their fall migrations huddle at night for warmth, often on the same trees used by previous generations.

Observers have built up strong evidence that many birds steer by the heavens. Yet navigating by the sun requires some kind of internal time sense in order to compensate for its movement across the sky. Experiments indicate that birds do indeed have a biological clock that enables them to hold a steady course. A tantalizing question remains as yet unanswered: How do these migrants know what their course should be? It's one thing to hold a steady course; it's another matter entirely to decide what course to hold.

Many creatures of land, water, and air seem to have this ability to steer by the sun: ants, bees, fishes, even the lumbering green turtles that navigate 1,400 miles from Brazil to tiny Ascension Island with pinpoint accuracy.

Some birds may be able to sense the earth's magnetic field and use it as a compass. To test this possibility, migrants were fitted with small magnets that warp the earth's magnetic lines. The intention was to throw the birds off course. Radar was used to plot each bird's course, but results were too sketchy for a firm conclusion.

For most birds, migration is a long haul, heavy with danger and physical stress. Before take-off they must fuel up with reserves of fat sometimes amounting to nearly half their total weight—no small task for a tiny dynamo such as the hummingbird. Many species span the Gulf of Mexico twice a year, unable to rest or feed until they reach land again. The folk of Yucatan often find new arrivals sprawled on the beaches, too exhausted to resist being picked up.

Blackpoll warblers fly over 2,100 miles of the Atlantic, passing by Bermuda without a stop as they wing from the coasts of Canada and New England to South America. Even a light headwind can spell disaster. Once the fat reserves are gone, the bird's body actually begins to convert its own muscles into the energy it needs to keep the wings beating. With luck it falls to the beach emaciated but alive; without, it becomes a small splash and a meal for a fish.

Most long-haul migrants land at intervals en route to rest and feed. Thus, on each trek, the migrant gambles that it can find food, spot a safe place to roost, and avoid whatever predators may be abroad. Flocks also seem to time their flights to take advantage of helping winds, letting an autumn cold front pass, for example, so they can ride the northerly breezes behind it. But like all weathermen, they sometimes guess wrong. Nearly a million dead Lapland longspurs were found in Minnesota as dawn broke after one sudden nighttime blizzard.

Faced with such enormous risks, why did the migrant species ever develop their wandering ways? One theory suggests that they are simply returning to ancestral nesting grounds from which they were driven by the glaciers. But, for all we know, migration may have been a well-established habit long before the Ice Age. Also, it is unlikely that a territorial memory would have persisted in a given species while it waited thousands of years for the ice to melt. And finally, many migratory species probably evolved in or near the tropics and, when they wing north to nest, are leaving their primal home, not returning to it.

Another theory suggests that the southward movement is simply a flight from the cold of winter, a scurry ahead of the icy blasts to a place where balmier breezes blow. But many birds leave their summer range well before the chill sets in, triggered not by temperature changes but perhaps by the shortening span of daylight.

Bird migration is a complex matter; different species migrate at different times, in various ways, for an assortment of reasons, and no general explanation can gather all the variables under its roof. But a look at the nature of the tropics can suggest a possible cause.

Despite its wet and dry seasons, the tropical climate tends to remain about the same year round. Thus the natural food larder is fairly constant and so are the numbers of customers that feed on it. A temperate zone, on the other hand, can feed only a relatively small number of customers year-round. But in spring and summer it pours out a bountiful smorgasbord of hatching insects, burgeoning plants, scampering lizards, frogs, toads—and the robin's ill-timed earthworm and billions more like him. The bird that leaves the crowded tropics and rears its heirs amid such riches can support a much larger family. The trip involves great risk to the individual, but in evolutionary terms the investment must be worth it or the habit would never have developed.

For some wanderers, it is life's seasons and not the sun's that stir the urge to migrate. Anchored in the rafting weeds of the Sargasso Sea east of the Bermuda islands, a leaf-shaped little squirmer begins its life with a migration of thousands of miles. Swimming and drifting for two-and-a-half years, *Anguilla anguilla* rides the Gulf Stream to the shores of Europe. There it quits salt water for fresh; its body swells to cylindrical form as it matures into one of the familiar eels of the European rivers.

In a decade its knell begins to sound, drawing it back to the mother sea. The call to migrate is so strong that eels in land-locked waters will squirm across dew-covered fields in order to join a river leading to the sea. Returning to the Sargasso, they spawn and die and leave their seed to retrace the ancient itinerary.

African army ants sweep in columns across the forest floor at 100 feet per hour in search of prey, bivouacking after 17 days for the queen to lay eggs. Triggered by the first heavy snowfall, Canadian caribou trek southward to the taiga. Strong swimmers, they have been known to buck swift tides while crossing four-mile-wide straights.

For the American eel *(Anguilla rostrata)* life's pattern is much the same. It spawns in the Sargasso Sea (although in a different part), spends its early life in salt water, and matures in the fresh waters of American rivers.

Salmon in both Atlantic and Pacific enact the same drama in reverse; life is lived in salt water but begins and ends in fresh. Streaming down out of the rivers of Alaska, Canada, and the Pacific Northwest come the sockeye hatchlings, bound for the open sea where they will mature and circle in year-long round trips spanning the ocean's width. Life, too, comes full circle, and at its closing the salmon array themselves in bright red nuptial hues on the return journey. No one knows exactly how each salmon finds the same river, and perhaps even the same riffle, where it burst from its egg years before. Its supersensitive nostrils can pick out odors diluted as much as one part in a billion —but can it remember the subtle smell of its birthplace over the span of years? Whatever its guidance, the salmon's drive is one of the strongest in nature; it leaps dams, braves bears, and often wears its own fins to tatters in its unswerving struggle to return to its first home, to spawn, and to die.

We humans too have staged some fairly impressive migrations in our brief tenure here, speeding across the planet. Some groups of men today, living off the migratory reindeer, or livestock that regularly require fresh pasturage, migrate with their herds. But basically we are stay-at-homes. We are, at least, until the autumn evening when we hear the geese crying overhead and rush out to watch their undulating V's slowly drift southward in the sunset. And then, as we trudge back into the house, there comes that ancient itch right there in the soles of our feet.

David Robinson

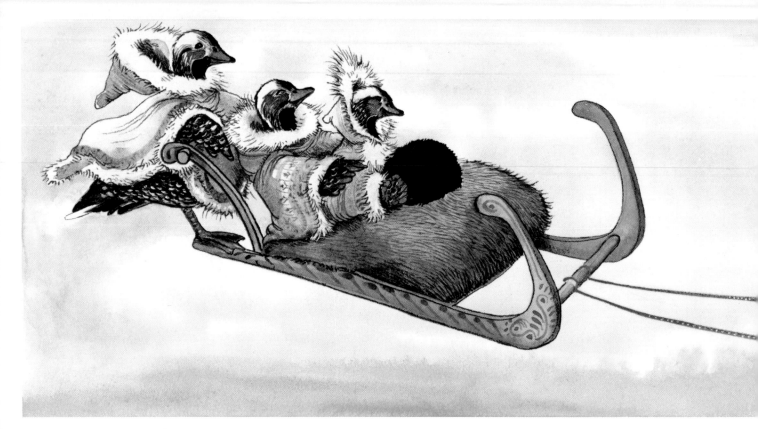

Mr. Crow Takes a Wife

Once upon a time there lived an old crow who was rather proud and puffed up about himself. Mr. Crow was as black as coal and in those days he had a long tail about which he was rather vain. He was unhappy, though, for he did not have a wife. Several of the birds he had asked to marry him had refused.

"We know you are quite wise, Mr. Crow, but we like grass and tender roots to eat. You hunt old dead things along the beach and you seldom eat the nice food we do. No, Mr. Crow," the birds replied, "we do not want to marry you."

So Mr. Crow was sad as fall came on and he saw the birds leaving to go south. He could see long strings of geese and other birds as they headed south, driving their bird sleds through the sky. He looked up, and coming right over him were Mr. White-fronted Goose and his family. The old gander was in front, pulling in the harness and, behind, his wife held the handle bars of the sled. The children were riding.

"Hello there, Mr. White-front," the old crow called. "Have you any daughters who would like to marry? I am looking for a wife and I would like to go south for the winter."

Mr. Goose looked down at Mr. Crow, but he kept on pulling away at his sky sled. "No, Mr. Crow," he replied, "my daughters are rather young to marry. Besides, you do not eat the things we do and

you would always be away, hunting along the seashore. That is a lovely boat you are building, but our girls do not need a boat; they can all swim." So the white-fronted geese went on their way.

Mr. Crow continued to work on his boat. He had an adz, a queer tool that all the Eskimo people use. They can take a round log and chop along it and make it up into boards. So the old crow worked on as another flock of geese came by. They were emperor geese, and Mr. Crow looked up at them. The old gander was pulling the sled and he leaned into the harness, for he was very strong. In the sled his one child, a girl goose, was riding. His wife was riding on the runners and holding the handle bars. They were really a beautiful family, with their pretty pearl-gray backs and their white heads.

"Hello, Mr. Emperor Goose," the old crow called to the family. "That is a beautiful daughter you have. Do you think she would care to marry me? I would like to go with you to the birdland for the winter."

Mr. Emperor Goose looked down at Mr. Crow, and the girl goose blushed. "I do not know, Mr. Crow. Maybe it will be all right if our daughter is willing. That is a fine kayak you are building; but she really needs none, for she can swim very well." The old gander stopped near Mr. Crow's igloo to talk it over. He took off the harness he wore while pulling the sky sled, and sat down on the grass.

"What do you think about it, Mama?" he asked Mrs. Emperor Goose.

"I suppose it is all right," she said, looking at Mr. Crow and his long tail. "He really is making a lovely kayak and he would not be such a bad-looking son-in-law. I am afraid, though, he would have trouble keeping up with us as we go to the birdland for the winter. We go very fast, for our sky sled is not heavily loaded. What if he should fall off as we cross the big wide ocean?"

"Oh, I am quite strong," Mr. Crow bragged and he arched his long tail. "I can pull the sky sled, myself, and I will not get tired when we cross the big wide ocean. Just wait until I put on my parka and my water boots and close the igloo door. I am all ready to leave."

Mr. Crow was so excited that he worked quickly. "What a lovely goose girl the young Emperor woman is," he thought. How he would show off before them when he took his turn pulling the sky sled! Soon Mr. Crow was all ready.

"You had better ride behind on the runners and hold the handle bars," Mr. Emperor Goose told the old crow. "It is really quite hard work and I do not think you are strong enough to do it."

"Nonsense," said Mr. Crow, putting on the harness. "I will pull the sled through the sky, and you ride on the runners, Mr. Goose, and hold onto the handle bars."

Mr. Crow set off as fast as he could go. He wanted to show the young goose girl how strong he was, and he pulled as hard as he could.

"**M**ercy," said Mrs. Emperor Goose, "we certainly are going fast! We should be to the big wide ocean tonight if we go this swiftly."

So the old crow pulled all the harder. They passed several families of other birds who were not pulling their sleds so fast. All of them were surprised to see Mr. Crow doing all the work.

After quite a distance the old crow grew tired. He had never been so fagged out in all his life. He was sorry, now, that he had not let Mr. Emperor Goose pull in the harness, and his wings hurt so that he could hardly go another foot.

"Here, Mr. Crow," the Emperor Goose said, "let me pull the sky sled."

"Oh, I can pull it, Mr. Goose," and the old crow spurted up a bit. "I really am very strong. I think I can pull the sled clear to the land where the birds live." He pulled all the harder, but he was getting very weak.

At last the old gander went up and took the harness from Mr. Crow. "You ride behind," he told him. "I will pull the sky sled for a while."

Poor Mr. Crow was so tired he was almost dead. His lovely tail, which had streamed out behind, now drooped down. He hung on to the handle bars, and Mr. Emperor Goose went like the wind. Soon they came to the big wide ocean and started right across. When they were halfway, they hit a rough cloud of air and the sky sled gave a terrible bounce.

The poor old crow fell right off behind. He was so tired that he could not even say a word, and on went Mr. Goose with the sled. Mrs. Emperor Goose and the daughter were looking ahead, enjoying the ride. They did not know that Mr. Crow had fallen off.

The old crow flapped his wings as strongly as he could but he kept getting lower in the sky. Soon he was only a few feet above the waves.

"Oh, I am going to drown," he thought, "and I was just going to marry the beautiful goose girl. Why did I ever act so foolish and try to pull the sky sled so fast?"

Mr. Crow could see the shore of the big wide ocean. But he just could not make it. At last a big wave touched his wing; then another touched his tail and—kerplop!—the old crow fell right into the water. The shore was only a few feet away.

How Mr. Crow did wish that he had learned to swim like the geese! He went clear down to the bottom. Giving a kick with his feet, up he came again. The salty water got into his nose and went down his throat. He choked terribly. Down he went again. Surely now he would drown. Just then a big wave washed Mr. Crow right out onto the sand.

For a long time Mr. Crow lay on the sand and gasped for breath. He had a stomach-ache. At last he sat up, took off his parka, and wrung the water out of it. Then he shook the water from his long tail and felt better. He rested again, then jumped into the air and followed along in the tracks that the sled had made in the sky. He must catch up with Mr. Goose and his lovely daughter.

After some time Mr. Crow saw the emperor geese. Fortunately, they had stopped their sled near a lot of other birds. He saw the white-fronted geese, the snow geese, and the black brants. Even the little sandpipers were there with a tiny sled, and Mr. King Eider Duck had a very fancy one made of walrus ivory.

"We were worried about you, Mr. Crow," Mr. Emperor Goose said. "What happened to you? I could not turn my sled around, for we were over the big wide ocean, but I knew that one so strong as you could get here all right by himself."

The old crow did not tell Mr. Emperor Goose what had happened, for he was rather ashamed of the way he had acted. Instead he asked, "What are all these birds waiting here for? Why don't we go ahead to the south?"

"It is the Canadian geese and the curlews," Mrs. Emperor Goose answered him. "They are always late. Each year we have had to wait for them here. You see, we all try to meet here and fly through the Clapping Mountains together."

Poor Mr. Crow, he was so tired! And when Mrs. Emperor Goose spoke of the Clapping Mountains, he felt worse. "Heavens," he thought, "I forgot all about the Clapping Mountains. They are likely to catch me this time, because I am so tired I cannot fly very fast." (Everyone feared the Clapping Mountains because the two high mountains stood very close together and frequently clapped together like the clapping of hands. Anyone caught between them would be crushed to death.)

At last Mr. Emperor Goose grew impatient. "I think I will go ahead," he told his wife. "I am tired of having to wait every year for the Canadian geese and the curlews." So Mr. Goose put on his pulling harness and Mrs. Goose and the goose girl got into the sled. "We must fly very hard," Mr. Emperor Goose said. "You, Mr. Crow, hold the handle bars, but do not ride on the runner. You had better flap your wings and help me to make more speed."

Away they went like the very wind.

Mr. Crow did the very best he could, but he could only flap feebly along. "Faster, Mr. Crow," the Emperor Goose called back. "We will be sure to be caught in the Clapping Mountains."

The big gander pulled very hard and Mr. Crow, hanging on to the handle bars, could barely even fly hard enough to keep up. His long tail streamed out behind, and he was badly frightened. Just as Mr. Emperor Goose got through the mountains, they began to tremble; in a second they clapped together as hard as they could. Mr. Crow gave a terrible squawk, for his long tail was caught between the straight walls. They cut his long feathers short, so that he did not have any more tail than a chicken.

How foolish Mr. Crow felt with his beautiful tail gone! The goose girl laughed, and that made him feel more silly than ever.

"If you ask me," said Mr. Emperor Goose, "it helps your looks decidedly not to have that silly tail waving out behind. What good was it anyway? It was only in the way and you could never swim with it on."

So the crow felt better. He found that it was easier to fly, and the goose girl smiled at him again.

When they reached the Aleutian Islands, Mr. Emperor Goose said that this was the place they would spend the winter. As soon as Mr. Crow had built an igloo, a great feast was held and Mr. Crow and the goose girl were married. Mr. Crow, by this time, had almost forgotten all about his nice long tail that he had lost up in the Clapping Mountains, and the other birds didn't seem to notice that he had lost it. Ever since that time, the crows have had short tails.

It is good for one always to try to pull his share of the load, but he should not be so silly as to think he can do it all.

Condensed from an Eskimo folk tale
as recorded by Charles E. Gillham

Bright Passage

S plashed among the reds, purples and rusts that bedeck the forest in autumn, the lemon-yellows of birch leaves add a lighter touch. It's really a matter of chemistry and climate. But when those leaves begin to turn, we humans turn to metaphor for an explanation. It's nature's paint-brush at work, we say.

Botanists tell us the colors were there all the time. The autumn hues, they say, are really an unmasking of colors that were hidden by the darker green of chlorophyll, the substance that uses light, carbon dioxide, and water to fab-ricate food for the plant.

The changes of the season really begin in late summer, when the shorter days make less light available. Longer nights and lower temperatures lead to the breakdown of chlorophyll. At the same time, a hormone at the base of each leaf stem, or petiole, begins to form a circlet of cork, the abcission layer, that weakens the connection until the leaf and tree part company.

Why, though, do birch leaves always turn yellow? Pri-marily because they contain an abundance of yellow pig-ment called xanthophyll. Colors in other trees come from chemicals with equally high-sounding names, like carotene (orange-yellow), anthocyanin (red) and tannin (brown).

The colors signify that the leaves are done with making food, but even after they flutter to the ground, they have yet another role to play: they protect the exposed ground from erosion and their decaying bulk replenishes the soil. Thus life, like the rhythm of the seasons, goes on.

Bill Vogt

The Sweetest Meat Grows on Trees

I f you doubt that the Good Old Days are still very much with us, you've been too long away from that pleasant country beyond the expressway where autumn still means, among other things, picking fallen hickory nuts out of the grass or filling a burlap bag with black walnuts.

Somehow, the nut trees have survived the changes in land use surprisingly well over the years and the eastern half of the United States is still amazingly rich in nut-bearing species. Small but sweet-meated beechnuts and hazelnuts are more common than generally known, and such favorites as pecans, black walnuts, butternuts and shellbarks, native to North America, are abundant and widespread.

The fact that you don't even own a single tree needn't doom the project. There are nut trees to spare in most areas, many utilized only by chipmunks and squirrels. While those on privately owned mountain lands and uncultivated farmlands are considered fair game in many areas, it's safer and more considerate to ask permission.

Equipment for nutting is simple and cheap. A burlap bag for the heavyweights—walnuts, pecans, or butternuts—and a basket or cloth feed bag for hickory nuts and the like.

Hickory trees (right) yield a rich larder of nuts the whole family enjoys harvesting. Like beechnuts (opposite, left) and pecans (opposite, right), hickory nuts drop after heavy frosts.

Nutting is not a matter of walking around looking for nuts; it's more a matter of looking for nut trees—which can be distinguished at greater distances. One of the easiest to learn to know is the stately shellbark, a tall, straight hickory that often stands alone in rich bottomlands. The bark is unmistakable—hard and gray, splitting into strips that curl from the trunk at both ends. The similar shagbark hickory is usually called shellbark, too, and except for its smaller nuts it is equally worthwhile. Both bear nuts in thick, four-parted hulls. Their fine flavor is a delight in cakes and cookies, or eaten *au naturel*.

A large and distinctly flavored hickory nut of more southern distribution is the celebrated pecan. It has been widely planted, but wild trees are found throughout much of the southern and central Mississippi Valley as well as Texas and the mountains of Mexico. Old trees attain imposing proportions, with a spreading crown and light brown or grayish furrowed bark. The familiar oblong nuts are encased in a thin husk that splits when ripe. No one who has eaten pecan "sticky-buns" or a properly concocted pecan pie needs to be told how these crisp kernels should be used.

Few trees furnish more handsome wood than the black walnut, and its nuts are likewise hard to beat. Their flavor is rich and robust, coming through unimpaired in cakes, cookies, nut bread and fudge. It is the nut supreme for sundaes. And black walnut trees are easy to spot. They are usually the first trees to drop their leaves in the fall, and you can see the spherical nuts clinging to the bare twigs like small, rough, greenish apples.

First cousin to the black walnut is the butternut, often called white walnut. It is a smaller tree and, when young, has smoother, slightly fissured, pale gray bark, and it often grows on higher ground. Its husk is coated with sticky hairs and the rough, extremely hard shells are studded with sharp spines. Butternuts have delicately flavored meats, but they are so thin and well protected by the thick, flinty shells that it is difficult to extract them in large pieces. Old-time nut-pickers soak a burlap bag partly filled with the butternuts in a tub of hot water for a half hour, and then hang them up to drain and cool. After that treatment they are easily cracked, and the meats come out in large pieces.

Less well known is the American hazelnut. It is produced by a shrub that grows along fencerows, in forest clearings, and in pasture clumps in the eastern half of the United States. The roundish, hard-shelled nuts are enclosed in a flaring, leaflike husk. They are as crisp and delicious as the larger, cultivated filbert.

Another generally unfamiliar native is the beechnut, the fruit of a large, forest tree with smooth, gray bark and leaves that often fade to near-white and, on young trees, cling to the branches all winter. Over much of its range the handsome beech does not bear fruit every year, and in some localities only rarely. But during a good year hordes of these diminutive, triangular nuts burst from husks beset with soft, recurved prickles. Their small size discourages their use, but the sweet flavor and soft shells that can be opened with the thumbnail make them an irresistible nibble.

If someone says nutting isn't what it used to be, he's right in one respect. The native chestnuts are gone. Once common in eastern forests, they were wiped out by an introduced fungus early in this century. Fortunately, saplings still sprout from the indomitable roots of these dead patriarchs and bear a small crop of nuts before succumbing to the "blight." A quart can often be gathered when the burrs split and drop them to the ground.

Large nuts should be permitted to dry thoroughly before storing. The thick, moist hulls of black walnuts are best removed in the field by grinding them underfoot. The common practice of exposing black walnuts to the weather until the hulls rot off generally results in shrunken, rubbery meats.

Butternuts and pecans have thin hulls that seldom present any difficulties, and shellbarks are easily freed of their hulls.

Most nuts keep better uncracked, but to save space you may prefer to crack them and store only the meats. Put them in closed jars or plastic boxes in a dry place, or in the refrigerator for extended storage.

Ned Smith

Hazelnuts (right) are so easily husked that nature often does it for you. In late summer, the ripe nuts frequently fall out of the outer hulls. Not so with black walnuts (left). To shuck them without cracking the shell, roll them underfoot or put them in a burlap bag and drive a car over it.

The possible uses of your autumn nut harvest would fill a good cookbook. The housewife who substitutes our native species for supermarket varieties will find them delightfully different.

Nut Casserole

1/3 cup raisins
1/3 cup finely chopped dried apricots
2 cups cooked brown rice
1½ cup unblanched almonds, slivered
or ground
½ cup butter, melted
sea salt to taste
1 tablespoon raw sugar or honey
Soak fruits in cold water to cover for 30 minutes. Drain. Preheat oven to 350°. Combine rice, fruits and nuts in an oiled casserole. Stir in butter, salt and sugar or honey. Bake 30 minutes or until firm. Yield: 6 servings.

Pralines

4 cups brown sugar, firmly packed
½ cup cream
2 tablespoons butter
2½ cups (1 pound) whole pecans
Combine sugar, cream, and butter in a saucepan; stir over medium heat until sugar dissolves. Bring to boiling point and boil 3 minutes, or until candy thermometer reads 240°, or a few drops form a soft ball in cold water. Remove from heat and let stand 5 minutes without stirring. Add nuts and stir until the syrup thickens and begins to look cloudy. Drop from tablespoon to make patties on a buttered cookie sheet. Let stand until cold. Makes 2 to 3 dozen.

Chestnut Stuffing Chimney Hill

3 cups chestnuts
¼ cup (½ stick) butter
¼ cup finely chopped onion
½ pound ground pork
¼ teaspoon sage
¼ teaspoon thyme
2 tablespoons finely chopped parsley
Gash chestnut tops, boil 35 minutes, shell, peel inner skins, and crumble lightly with fork. Melt butter in heavy skillet; simmer onions in it 5 minutes. Add pork and saute until slightly browned. Stir in sage, thyme, and parsley. Fold in chestnuts and mix well. Pack loosely into fowl. Makes enough for 8-pound bird.

Nut Salad Dressing

½ cup sesame seed oil
2 tablespoons olive oil
2 tablespoons lemon juice
1 tablespoon honey
juice of 1 orange
½ cup pecans or walnuts, chopped
Put the oils, lemon juice, honey, and juice of orange in a blender and blend for 40 seconds. Put in a bowl and add chopped nuts; chill until used. Serve with fresh fruit salads. Makes 1 cup.

Wonderful Walnut Pie Crust

1 cup finely ground walnuts or hickory
nuts
2½ tablespoons sugar
¼ teaspoon salt
Blend nuts, sugar and salt. Press with a spoon on bottom and sides of a buttered 8-inch pie pan. Bake at 400° for 6 to 8 minutes. Cool and fill with ice cream.

Hickory-Nut Brittle

¾ cup chopped hickory nuts
1 cup white sugar
½ cup brown sugar, firmly packed
¼ cup light corn syrup
½ cup water
2 tablespoons butter
pinch of baking soda
pinch of salt
Warm nuts in 275° oven. Combine white and brown sugars, corn syrup, and water in medium saucepan, and stir over low heat until sugar dissolves. Raise heat and cook without stirring until candy thermometer registers 300° to 310°, or until drops thread when falling from a spoon. Remove from stove, add butter, soda, salt, and warm nuts, stirring as little as possible. Turn at once onto buttered baking sheet. Quickly press candy into thin layer with spatula. When cool enough to handle, grasp edges with fingers, lift, and stretch to make sheet as thin as possible. When cold, crack into irregular pieces.

Filbert and Fruit Candy

7-ounce package pitted dates
¼ cup dried figs
1 cup filberts
1 cup white raisins
confectioner's sugar
1 tablespoon dark rum or bourbon
whiskey, optional
Put dates, figs, raisins, and nuts through food chopper, then blend ingredients. Shape resulting paste into about 15 balls and roll in powdered sugar. If fruits seem dry, mix in up to 1 tablespoon rum or bourbon.

The Day We Smoked the Bee Tree

I t was a drowsy summer afternoon. I'd moved my work to an elm-shaded porch where a view of thunderheads gathering above the distant Alleghenies gave promise of relief in the offing. Then I heard them. They came scrambling over the pasture fence, their eager young voices barely audible above the deep-throated barking of Nanny, their ever-present St. Bernard companion. "We found it! We found it!"

It, I knew at once, was the bee tree. The search had begun three weeks before, shortly after that June day when our family took up residence in the large farmhouse in Lahmansville, West Virginia, that would be our home for the next year. To my two New Mexico-reared children, James, 12, and Becky, 10, this land of verdant valleys and dense forests was a world apart. Most fascinating, to them, were the bees. Enchanted, they sat for hours watching as the tiny creatures penetrated the deep throat of each flower, then, abruptly, darted out of sight.

One afternoon I remarked, "Well, there's a bee tree around here somewhere."

Bee lines really work. Once bees find the honey box you have set out, they return to it about the same time each day, using landmarks to help orient themselves. With patience it is possible to follow them back to their hive.

"A bee tree?" They were puzzled, and the stage was set for a long discussion about honeybees.

Drawing on my boyhood experiences in Kentucky, I explained how hunting for wild honey was once an important event for many families. Honey was a major staple. Honeycomb, boiled down to beeswax, was a basic ingredient in the important production of candles.

"But how do you find a bee tree?" James asked.

"One of the best ways is to use a honey box," I replied. "You fill a small open box with honey and set it outside. Worker bees will gorge on the honey and carry it to their hive. You sight their direction of flight against a distant tree or rock. That's a 'bee line.' You gradually work your way along the bee line, moving the honey box as you go. Eventually, the workers will lead you right to their hive."

Next morning we constructed a honey box from a small candy tin, set in a wooden shell. Then, over my wife's mild protests, we poured in a half pint of honey we found in the pantry.

We set the box atop a post in the garden. By afternoon James and Becky had moved the honey box to the pasture. By sunset they'd established a firm leg of their bee line to a low hill nearby.

And so it went. Early each morning they were off with Nanny to hunt for the bee tree. Sometimes a leg of the bee line would prove false and they'd backtrack and start again. By the second week, they entered the thick forest on the back side of the farm, nearly a mile away. It was there that sweltering day they successfully concluded their hunt and came running home.

We went at once to study their find. Deep in the shaded forest, an ancient maple stood rooted near the crest of a low hummock. Deprived of sun by the greater oaks surrounding it, the tree was stunted and gnarled. At the base of its rotted trunk was a hole the size of a basketball. Higher up about six feet from the ground, was a smaller, pear-sized hole, where a steady traffic of bees entered and emerged, their busy flight clearly audible in the still forest. Indeed, this was the bee tree.

"But how do we get the honey?" James asked, concerned about the retaliation of aroused bees.

"We'll smoke them," I replied. "With straw and burlap."

"Hey!" they shouted.

"Not yet," I said. "This fall, when the weather's cold and the bees are dormant."

A look of disappointment crossed their faces. "It won't be long," I said.

Fall comes brilliantly to Appalachia. By mid-October, when the mountains were blanketed in scarlet and gold, it was time to smoke the bee tree. One Saturday morning, following proven precautions, we showered carefully and dressed in our lightest colored clothing. After breakfast we checked our equipment. There was a dry gunny sack, some damp straw, a few small wads of burlap, a galvanized tub, an ax, a saw, a hammer and nails, and some large spoons. Against my better judgment I included Nanny.

An old logging road let us drive to within 25 yards of the bee tree. The forest was still, with only a hint of a breeze, near perfect conditions for our purpose. Using the station wagon tailgate for a table, we put the wads of burlap and some of the wet straw into the sack and rolled it all loosely into a ball. Then we shoved the homemade smudge pot into the hole at the base of the tree and lighted the sack.

"Will it kill them?" Becky asked apprehensively.

"No," I reassured her. "Just quiet them . . . I hope."

We retreated a few yards. "Stand perfectly still," I said. Then, to Nanny, who was intently watching our every move, I commanded: "Sit!" She obeyed immediately.

Soon, a stale, musty odor filled the autumn-crisp air. Moments later a thin wisp of blue-black smoke escaped from the small, higher hole and curled upward through the frosted leaves.

"Look!" James shouted. A number of bees, aroused from the inactive center of the dormant cluster, emerged from the smaller hole and buzzed angrily near our heads. Becky began to swat.

"No!" I warned sharply. "That'll get you stung. Stand. . . ."

Before I could finish, a loud "Woof!" interrupted me. With a lunge, Nanny, her curiosity overcoming her obedience, charged the tree, stood upright against the trunk and barked furiously at the smoke wisping from the upper hole. It was all the enticement the angry bees needed. They dived for the hapless dog's head. With howls of pain and surprise she dropped to all fours. Then, with bounding leaps she covered the distance from the tree to where we were parked, clambered onto the lowered tailgate and disappeared into the station wagon.

In a moment James said laconically, "I bet she learned something that time." In hearty agreement, we laughed.

When at last the old tree was quiet, we raked out the still-smoldering smudge and stomped the embers. "Now, we'll probe," I said. I sawed a plug from the tree about two feet from the ground. We spotted the honeycomb at once. James and Becky shouted their delight. But I shook my head. The honey was dark, surely too bitter for our taste.

I cut a second plug, higher up. Here the comb was light amber. "This is better," I said. I sawed a horizontal cut at the plug and another a couple of feet higher. Then, with the ax, I cut downward from each end of the upper cut to the same end of the lower cut. When I pried away the wood we had a window directly into the hive and its lode of golden honeycomb.

I saw that the hive extended far above our opening. The old tree, I estimated, held at least 150 pounds of honey, far more than we wanted. "That's good," I said, "Never take all the honey from a wild hive unless you take the bees, too, or they'll starve."

With the large spoons we dislodged the honeycomb and put it into the tub. In half an hour we'd gathered about 65 pounds. With the comb strained out, that would make about 20 quarts, plenty for us and enough for friends.

While James and Becky licked the spoons, I replaced the wood over the opening and nailed it tight. Soon, the hive would return to peaceful dormancy with plenty of food to sustain it.

We set the heavy tub in the rear of the wagon and drove home, full of cheer for a job well done. At the house I backed close to the rear porch so we could carry the tub directly into the kitchen. "Get your mother," I said.

I went to the cellar for something to prop the back door open. Then, suddenly, I heard my wife cry out, "Oh, no!" I rushed up the steps. Dumbfounded, they stood staring into the rear of the station wagon. There, like some gluttonous hog at a just-filled trough, Nanny was gobbling honey and comb as fast as she could. It was too late to stop her. What she couldn't eat, certainly no one else would. With a sigh of dejection I sat down.

We were all momentarily silent. Then Becky came and sat down beside me. "Daddy," she said. "I guess she's just getting even."

We all exchanged glances. Then we looked back at Nanny. She had both front feet in the tub now. Suddenly, at the sight of a 200-pound shaggy dog matted from head to toe with gooey honey, we began to laugh. It became infectious. Holding our sides, we laughed until we could laugh no more.

After we had locked a miserable dog in the barn, James and Becky excitedly recounted the day's events to their mother. They spoke of "honey boxes" and "bee lines" and "smudges." And, as I listened, an awareness grew in me. In the past few weeks, I realized, my children had momentarily entered an era that is quickly vanishing from the American scene. The bittersweet thought both pleased and saddened me. But, no matter what the future brought, I knew that they would never forget this rollicking, fun-filled day—the day we smoked the bee tree.

William J. Buchanan

Smoking a bee tree makes collecting its wild honey a much safer venture. The bees react as if their hive were on fire and, after an initial frenzy, concentrate on engorging themselves with honey preparatory to making their escape. Most of them are so busy that they don't guard the hive and are less likely to sting.

Hallowe'en

This is Hallowe'en

Goblins on the doorstep,
  Phantoms in the air,
Owls on witches' gateposts
  Giving stare for stare,
Cats on flying broomsticks,
  Bats against the moon,
Stirrings round of fate-cakes
  With a solemn spoon,
Whirling apple parings,
  Figures draped in sheets
Dodging, disappearing,
  Up and down the streets,
Jack-o'-lanterns grinning,
  Shadows on a screen,
Shrieks and starts and laughter—
—This is Hallowe'en!

Dorothy Brown Thompson

Hallowe'en Indignation Meeting

A sulky witch and a surly cat
And a scowly owl and a skeleton sat
With a grouchy ghost and a waspish bat,
And angrily snarled and chewed the fat.

It seems they were all upset and riled
That they couldn't frighten the Modern Child,
Who was much too knowing and much too wild
And considered Hallowe'en spooks too mild.

Said the witch, "They call this the *human* race,
Yet the kiddies inhabit Outer Space;
They bob for comets, and eat ice cream
From flying saucers, to get up steam!"

"I'm a shade of my former self," said the skeleton.
"I shiver and shake like so much gelatin,
Indeed I'm a pitiful sight to see—
I'm scareder of *kids* than they are of *me*!"

Margaret Fishback

Cider

No drink is closer to this country's traditions than the juice of the apple. "Cider is to be found in every house," wrote an 18th-century Hudson Valley farmer. "Our cider," he added, "affords the degree of exhilaration with which we are satisfied."

Nowadays, in this era of improvements—sometimes gratuitous ones—apple juice is pasteurized for mass distribution. But this cannot compare with authentic, old-fashioned cider. Pressed from the surplus of the orchard harvest and allowed to mature with unhasty grace, developing more character every day, cider remains one of the most satisfying liquid refreshments devised by man.

The first American cider was made the same way good natural cider is made today. When the autumn air is crisp and the ripened fruit has mel-

lowed until "at thirty feet distance you catch the fragrant apple aroma" (said the Shaker orchardists who were famous for the quality they achieved), the apples are gathered, crushed or chopped, and put through a press. As the golden juice cascades out under the power of the screw or other squeezing device, it is poured into containers and then stored in a cool place. Until it begins to ferment, it is known as sweet cider; and until it sours into vinegar—that is, while it retains tiny bubbles and has a pleasant tang—it is hard cider, a slightly alcoholic drink that once was more common than milk on American tables.

John Adams downed a tankard of hard cider before breakfast every morning until his death at the age of ninety-one. In Pennsylvania, naturalist John Bartram's homemade cider

was so good that Ben Franklin habitually visited him to hoist a mug or two. Later, during the "Log Cabin and Hard Cider" campaign of 1840, when William Henry Harrison was derided in the press as a frontiersman deserving of no more than a soldier's pension, a log cabin, and a barrel of cider, his partisans turned the slur to their advantage. Log-cabin clubs cropped up all over the country; hard cider was lavished on voters; and incumbent Martin Van Buren's princely preference for champagne was made to seem un-American. Cider turned the voice of the common man to song:

Let Van from his coolers of silver
drink wine,
And lounge on his cushioned settee.
Our man on his buckeye bench can
recline,
Content with hard cider is he! . . .

Contentment is only one of the promises inherent in cider. It has become the basis of many popular concoctions, including apple champagne, which might well have satisfied Van Buren. This pale sparkling drink is made by adding equal parts of white and brown sugar to freshly pressed apple juice. The mixture is allowed to fizz for eight weeks in a cool place and then siphoned into bottles that are capped and marked with the date of pressing. Another spirit, the most potent and the least adulterated of American cider variations, used to be made—and still can be—by leaving a bucket of hard cider outdoors when the thermometer dropped below freezing. The watery part of the effervescent juice turns to ice, leaving a slightly oily brandy sometimes called applejack (a term also

given to the highly potent cider brandy distilled from apples).

Both hard cider and applejack are sold in many liquor stores, and good cider is imported from England and France by vintners. But the best American cider is found in our own orchard country. Here, at the few rural cider mills that still come to life in the fall, operators press their own apples or the fruit brought by customers. Fermentation of fresh cider begins at once, unless it is pasteurized or otherwise tainted with additives.

Cider has been called the *vin du pays* of America, and, like any good wine, it has been recognized as a boon

Horse- and man-powered cider mills were common in rural America in 1870 when William Davis painted this scene.

to cooking. Amelia Simmons, who in 1796 compiled what she called America's first cookbook, prescribed hard cider for use in the frothy libation known as syllabub. Other traditional recipes include dozens of cooked dishes that cry out for the tang of old-fashioned cider. A specialty of the Pennsylvania Dutch is a spicy cider soup, and a dessert once popular with Shaker cooks in Ohio combined apple omelets with sweet cider sauce. Herbed trout poached in cider and served with a buttery cider sauce gained fame as a Philadelphia favorite, and some soul-food cooks boil pigs' feet in apple juice. Ham, of course, is often simmered in the liquid , and there are cider-flavored pot roasts.

Old recipes for mincemeat, meat glazes, pie, and posset—a hot spiced drink—often call for boiled cider. This is simply fresh cider, neither pasteurized nor chemically stabilized, whose flavor is heightened by boiling the liquid to reduce it to one half or one quarter of its original volume. Traditionally, boiled cider was made outdoors immediately after the apple juice was extracted. Where there were no cider mills, horses were hitched to poles and walked in a circle all day long to turn the wheels of the apple crusher. The juice was poured into a huge iron kettle hung from a tripod straddling a wood fire, and neighboring women gathered to take turns stirring with long wooden paddles until the product looked like light molasses. They scalded jars to bottle and seal some of the boiled liquid, or they turned part of it into another big kettle and added pared, cored, and quartered apples to prepare applesauce or apple butter. The butter made a sweet and spicy spread for bread; and boiled-cider applesauce, one New Hampshire woman remembered, "was generally used in a two-crust pie which was a perfect finale for any meal!"

Whether cider is incorporated in a recipe or served as a drink, its flavor enhances just about everything. Mark Twain, who is known as an eloquent apologist for his native foods, was never more tender than when he remembered that "cider and doughnuts make old people's old tales and old jokes sound fresh . . . enchanting, and juggle an evening away before you know what went with the time."

Evan Jones

MCINTOSH
salads and baking

WINESAP
cooking and baking

DELICIOUS
salads, eating raw

JONATHAN
cooking and baking

GOLDEN DELICIOUS
salads and cooking

ROME BEAUTY
cooking and baking

RHODE ISLAND GREENING
cooking and baking

How to Make Your Own Cider

1. A bushel of apples produces one to two gallons of cider. Any kind of apples may be used, but experts prefer a combination of varieties; for example, Rome Beauties for sweetness, McIntoshes for aroma, and Winesaps for tang. Apples left on the ground produce cider with an earthy taste, unripe ones are too starchy.
2. After picking, let the apples rest a day or so to gather juice and flavor; then scrub them and cut out wormholes and decay. Keep the fruit, equipment, and working area clean.
3. Before pressing the apples, grind, chop, or crush them into a fine pulp. If you don't have a grinder or a press with a grinder attachment like the one shown on page 101, use a food chopper, apple grater, or slaw cutter.
4. For small amounts of cider you can put the pulp into a porous cloth bag and, with someone's help, wring the juice into a vat or tub. For larger amounts you will need a press. To keep the cider free of particles, line the slatted container with a clean cloth. Then fill it with pulp. Next fold over the edges of the cloth and press the pulp at once by turning the rod slowly.
5. Catch the juice from the press in a pail covered with cheesecloth, which acts as a strainer. It can be drunk immediately but tastes better if left in a cool place for a few days.
6. For hard cider let the liquid ferment slowly at a temperature not above 50 degrees.

Where to Buy a Cider Press

Old presses—often in need of renovation—frequently turn up for sale. Several manufacturers make new presses for home use: Garden Way Research, Charlotte, VT 05445, sells a press and grinder for $189.50, do-it-yourself kits for $64.50; Berarducci Bros., 1900 Fifth Ave., McKeesport, PA 15132, has a small model without grinder for $37.50, larger ones up to $420; MacKay's Wood Products, P.O. Box 1023, Bellingham, WA 98225, offers a mill (grinder and press, grinder run by electric motor) for $293.50 and kits starting at $73.75; Sears' catalog sells a hand-turned fruit crusher for $67.95; Montgomery Ward's catalog offers one for $44.99 that presses 60 lbs. of fruit.

Bringing Out the Beast

In the gastronomical good old days wildlife graced almost every table. Indeed, game provided a mainstay of the American diet, and people on the frontier probably didn't realize how lucky they were to have succulent game almost as daily fare. Today, wildlife meats are luxuries—a game farm mallard duck costs more than five dollars a pound. When I was a youngster growing up on the Great Plains, game was the fall-time staple. The daily limit of prairie chickens, grouse and ducks was fifteen each, and four Canada geese. Shotgun shells cost a little over a dollar for twenty-five in those days, shooting was permitted on practically anyone's land and one had to be a poor marksman not to get his limit.

The result was that we ate game birds from the opening of the season in September until the closing, usually in December, of the southern migration of birds hatched and grown in Canada. Then, in winter, cottontail rabbits were popular table fare. There was no big game in the vicinity.

Prairie chickens and grouse, virtually the same fowl, abounded. Several methods of hunting them were practical, but my parents were relaxed shooters.

They hitched up Old Snip to a single-seat buggy, and Touser, a pointer with some other blood, was sent out in front. When Touser pointed, my parents jumped out of the buggy. As the birds were flushed, they fired away, my father with a Parker 12-gauge double, my mother with a 20-gauge Parker double. She took the high deflection shots better than my father. I started out with a 16-gauge Remington pump gun, and did less well than my parents.

I often hunted prairie chickens alone on foot, for almost out of our back door prairie stretched for miles, and grain field stubble extended across the great aching spaces to the horizon—perfect land for game birds. The crisp autumn air was spiked with wisps of smoke from burning straw, for the harvest was in. I'd hike until I flushed a bird or covey.

Duck shooting was also great sport. In my youth, the Great Plains were dotted with sloughs, potholes and tiny lakes, some fed by creeks, pronounced "cricks," so clean and clear that one drank out of them. Mallards and teal nested in the reed-filled waters and brought up their young there. This was long before the agribarons drained sloughs and the highway lobby turned the engineers loose to crosshatch the natural landscape with tangles of concrete ribbons.

Legal duck shooting began at sunrise. Usually we would get up at 4 a.m., pull on long johns, woolen socks, rubber hip boots and a warm shooting jacket, then pile into a Model T with others, and set forth in the dark. The headlights blinked on the gravel roads, then dirt trails that ended at the slough. There we gathered shocks of grain and carried them, some over the barrels of our guns, through mud and water to clumps of tall reeds where we dumped the shocks to sit on, and then put out our wooden decoys and waited for the dawn.

Then the mallards flew in from their morning feeding, or ducks from other potholes glided in, all with a whistling of wing feathers. Most of the shooting was easy, almost straight on, but always there were some fast and high-flying birds, and some that demanded high deflection, which made for skillful shooting. There was plenty of action, but even during the lulls, just being in the open generated euphoria.

By about 10:30 or 11, no birds were flying—the coots or mud hens, which some gastronomes like, were considered beneath us, and so we broke off the encounter and waded to shore after picking up our ducks or having them fetched by a retriever.

The lunch everyone carried was rough and ready. Prohibition reigned, so the cocktail was a shot of "alkie" flavored with dubious things such as fake raspberry juice. The accompanying sandwiches were usually of home-baked bread, generously buttered and filled with slices of cold wild duck or prairie chicken. Sometimes a hunter brought along home brew, but he was lucky if it hadn't exploded while being jounced over the rough roads.

Getting back to today's reality, commercial game is usually frozen, and much of it (imports aside) is grown on game farms. There's no denying that birds and animals produced under such conditions lack the complete gamy taste of their wild counterparts, but still they are highly palatable. One must also remember that wild creatures get much more exercise than domesticated ones. This means they have less fat, which must be compensated for by larding or covering with slices of fat such as fresh or salt pork. Also, game tends to be chewy, so you may want to marinate some birds (such as old geese) and cuts of furred game, and then braise them. But I would rather chew a bit more than soak the game in a vinegar solution, or parboil it and thereby dilute the wild taste. Nor would I want to use a tenderizer as some books recommend.

The degree of doneness, especially for wild fowl, is a matter of taste, especially for ducks.

One shouldn't be frightened about cooking game. It's no more difficult than preparing domesticated birds and animals. In the recipes that follow, nothing more than standard cooking equipment is required, and if you have a penchant for a particular herb, sage for instance, let your palate be your guide. (Be sure to save carcasses for making a broth that is superb as a cooking liquid or as consomme.)

Great Plains Prairie Chicken

This game-bird recipe, from memory, was popular on the Great Plains, but especially for old prairie chickens and grouse. The age of the birds was judged by the pliability of their beaks (the older the stiffer).

1 prairie chicken or grouse
1 each medium onion, carrot and stalk of celery, all minced
salt and pepper
½ teaspoon dried sage
2 tablespoons butter
1 cup game or chicken stock

Season fowl inside and out and put sage and vegetables in the cavity. (Truss if you wish.) Brown bird in hot butter. Place fowl in casserole with tight fitting cover. Add stock. Bring casserole contents to boil on top of stove, then put in 350° oven for about 1½ to 2 hours, basting, and adding stock if necessary. Remove bird from vessel; the breast should come off easily in two pieces and be cooked entirely through. Skim fat from casserole liquid and discard. Serve liquid with the fowl. Serves 2.

Roast Duck

Whether to hang ducks depends on one's taste: two to four days in a cool place will result in slightly "high" fowl, which means it is gamier than a bird just killed. My preference is on the high side.

1 wild duck
gin
3 tablespoons soft butter
salt, freshly ground black pepper, leaves from one bunch of celery and one stalk minced
½ cup game or chicken stock

Wipe bird inside and out with a cloth soaked in gin and wrung out. Season inside and out with salt and pepper. Put celery leaves and stalk in cavity of duck and close opening. Coat breast-up duck with butter. Roast in preheated 500° oven for 18-20 minutes. Detach legs, slash them across on one side in several places and broil, cut side down, to desired doneness.

Slice breast thinly, laying slices in pan juices for a few minutes. Remove breast slices and deglaze pan with stock. Serve slices and legs with pan juices. Serves 2.

Roast Canada Goose McDaniel

This recipe is by Washington's gastronomical guru, Robert J. McDaniel.

1 Canada goose of 6 to 10 pounds
½ cup butter
1 cup finely minced onion
2 cups dry white wine
2 dozen freshly shucked select-size oysters and their liquor
½ teaspoon nutmeg
½ teaspoon dried tarragon
1 teaspoon paprika
½ cup freshly chopped parsley
½ teaspoon cayenne pepper
3 to 4 cups dry breadcrumbs
¼ pound salt pork cut in thin slices
1 ounce brandy or bourbon
1 ounce sherry
salt and freshly ground pepper
1 cup thick cream or sour cream (optional)

Melt butter in pan, add onion and stir over medium heat until onion begins to brown. Add the liver, heart and gizzard, sauteing until lightly browned. Add wine, cover pan and simmer gently for 20 minutes. Remove liver, heart and gizzard and reserve for gravy; save remaining liquid for basting.

In another pan, simmer oysters in part of their liquor for 5 minutes. Add remaining liquor with nutmeg, tarragon, parsley, paprika and cayenne and blend breadcrumbs carefully into this mixture.

Dampen goose with bourbon or brandy and sprinkle with salt and pepper inside and out. Stuff goose with oyster mixture and cover breast with salt pork slices. Place bird breast up in large roasting pan and put in preheated 450° oven. After 15 minutes reduce heat to 350° and baste frequently with liquid saved from giblet broth. Continue to roast, allowing 20 minutes per pound. Remove salt pork from breast for the last 20 minutes.

Remove goose. Skim fat from pan juices and add minced liver, heart and gizzard with the sherry and about ½ cup water. Stir over low heat until gravy is slightly thick, and stir in cream if desired. Serve gravy with slices of the goose. Serves 6.

Donald Dresden

Hunting the Deceitful Turkey

When I was a boy my uncle and his big boys hunted with the rifle, the youngest boy Fred and I with a shotgun—a small single-barrelled shotgun which was properly suited to our size and strength; it was not much heavier than a broom. We carried it turn about, half an hour at a time. I was not able to hit anything with it, but I liked to try; Fred and I hunted feathered small game, the others hunted deer, squirrel, wild turkeys, and such things. My uncle and the big boys were good shots. They killed hawks and wild geese and such like on the wing. . . .

In the first faint gray of the dawn the stately wild turkeys would be stalking around in great flocks, and ready to be sociable and answer invitations to come and converse with other excursionists of their kind. The hunter concealed himself and imitated the turkey-call by sucking the air through the leg-bone of a turkey which had previously answered a call like that and lived only just long enough to regret it. There is nothing that furnishes a perfect turkey call except that

Like most wild turkeys, this fine female has flown to her roost in late afternoon. Once roosted, these usually wily and elusive birds are not easily disturbed, even by people passing under the tree.

bone. Another of Nature's treacheries, you see. She is full of them; half the time she doesn't know which she likes best—to betray her child or protect it. In the case of the turkey she is badly mixed; she gives it a bone to be used in getting it into trouble, and she also furnishes it with a trick for getting itself out of the trouble again. When a mamma-turkey answers an invitation and finds she has made a mistake in accepting it, she does as the mamma-partridge does—remembers a previous engagement and goes limping and scrambling away, pretending to be very lame; and at the same time she is saying to her not-visible children, "Lie low, keep still, don't expose yourselves; I shall be back as soon as I have beguiled this shabby swindler out of the country."

When a person is ignorant and confiding, this immoral device can have tiresome results. I followed an ostensibly lame turkey over a considerable part of the United States one morning because I believed in her and could not think she would deceive a mere boy, and one who was trusting her and considering her honest. I had the single-barrelled shotgun, but my idea was to catch her alive. I often got within rushing distance of her, and then made my rush; but always, just as I made my final plunge and put my hand down where her back had been, it wasn't there; it was only two or three inches from there and I brushed the tail-feathers as I landed on my stomach—a very close call, but still not quite close enough; that is, not close enough for success, but just close enough to convince me that I could do it next time. She always waited for me, a little piece away, and let on to be resting and properly fatigued; which was a lie, but I believed it, for I still thought her honest long after I ought to have begun to doubt her, suspecting that this was no way for a high-minded bird to be acting. I followed, and followed, and followed, making my periodical rushes, and getting up and brushing the dust off, and resuming the voyage with patient confidence; indeed, with a confidence which grew, for I could see by the change of climate and vegetation that we were getting up into the high latitudes, and as she always looked a little tireder and a little more discouraged after each rush, I judged that I

was safe to win, in the end, the competition being purely a matter of staying power and the advantage lying with me from the start because she was lame.

Along in the afternoon I began to feel fatigued myself. Neither of us had had any rest since we first started on the excursion, which was upwards of ten hours before, though latterly we had paused awhile after rushes, I letting on to be thinking about something else; but neither of us sincere, and both of us waiting for the other to call game but in no real hurry about it, for indeed those little evanescent snatches of rest were very grateful to the feelings of us both; it would naturally be so, skirmishing along like that ever since dawn and not a bite in the mean time; at least for me, though sometimes as she lay on her side fanning herself with a wing and praying for strength to get out of this difficulty, a grasshopper happened along whose time had come, and that was well for her, and fortunate, but I had nothing—nothing the whole day.

More than once, after I was very tired, I gave up taking her alive, and was going to shoot her, but I never did it, although it was my right, for I did not believe I could hit her; and besides, she always stopped and posed, when I raised the gun, and this made me suspicious that she knew about me and my marksmanship, and so I did not care to expose myself to remarks.

I did not get her, at all. When she got tired of the game at last, she rose from almost under my hand and flew aloft with the rush and whir of a shell and lit on the highest limb of a great tree and sat down and crossed her legs and smiled down at me, and seemed gratified to see me so astonished.

I was ashamed, and also lost; and it was while wandering the woods hunting for myself that I found a deserted log cabin and had one of the best meals there that in my life-days I have eaten. The weed-grown garden was full of ripe tomatoes, and I ate them ravenously, though I had never liked them before. Not more than two or three times since have I tasted anything that was so delicious as those tomatoes. I surfeited myself with them, and did not taste another one until I was in middle life.

Mark Twain

The First Thanksgiving

A letter to a friend in England from Edward Winslow, a Mayflower pilgrim and later governor of the Plymouth colony, "setting forth a brief and true declaration of the worth of that plantation."

Loving and Old Friend,

You shall understand that in this little time that a few of us have been here, we have built seven dwelling-houses and four for the use of the plantation, and have made preparation for divers others. We set the last spring some twenty acres of Indian corn, and sowed some six acres of barley and pease; and according to the manner of the Indians, we manured our ground with herrings, or rather shads, which we have in great abundance, and take with great ease at our doors. Our corn did prove well; and, God be praised, we had a good increase of Indian corn, and our barley indifferent good, but our pease not worth the gathering, for we feared they were too late sown. They came up very well, and blossomed; but the sun parched them in the blossom.

Our harvest being gotten in, our governor sent four men on fowling, that so we might, after a special manner, rejoice together after we had gathered the fruit of our labors. They four in one day killed as much fowl as, with a little help beside, served the company almost a week. At which time, amongst other recreations, we exercised our arms, many of the Indians coming amongst us, and among the rest their greatest king, Massasoyt, with some ninety men, whom for three days we entertained and feasted; and they went out and killed five deer, which they brought to the plantation, and bestowed on our governor, and upon the captain and others. And although it be not always so plentiful as it was at this time with us, yet by the goodness of God we are so far from want, that we often wish you partakers of our plenty.

We have found the Indians very faithful in their covenant of peace with us, very loving, and ready to pleasure us. We often go to them, and they come to us. Some of us have been fifty miles by land in the country with them. . . . Yea, it hath pleased God so to possess the Indians with a fear of us and love unto us, that not only the greatest king amongst them, called Massasoyt, but also all the princes and peoples round about us, have either made suit unto us, or been glad of any occasion to make peace with us; so that seven of them at once have sent their messengers to us to that end. Yea, an isle at sea, which we never saw, hath also, together with the former, yielded willingly to be under the protection and subject to our sovereign lord King James. So that there is now great peace amongst the Indians themselves, which was not formerly, neither would have been but for us; and we, for our parts, walk as peaceably and safely in the wood as in the highways in England. We entertain them familiarly in our houses, and they as friendly bestowing their venison on us. They are a people without any religion or knowledge of any God, yet very trusty, quick of apprehension, ripe-witted, just. The men and women go naked, only a skin about their middles.

For the temper of the air here, it agreeth well with that in England; and if there be any difference at all, this is somewhat hotter in summer. Some think it to be colder in winter; but I cannot out of experience so say. The air is very clear, and not foggy, as hath been reported. I never in my life remember a more seasonable year than we have here enjoyed; and if we have once but kine, horses, and sheep, I make no question but men might live as contented here as in any part of the world. For fish and fowl, we have great abundance. Fresh cod in the summer is but coarse meat with us. Our bay is full of lobsters all the summer, and affordeth variety of other fish. In September we can take a hogshead of eels in a night, with small labor, and can dig them out of their beds all the winter. We have mussels and other [shellfish] at our doors. Oysters we have none near, but we can have them brought by the Indians when we will. All the spring-time the earth sendeth forth naturally very good sallet herbs. Here are grapes, white and red, and very sweet and strong also; strawberries, gooseberries, raspas, &c.; plums of three sorts, white, black, and red, being almost as good as a damson; abundance of roses, white, red and damask; single, but very sweet indeed. The country wanteth only industrious men to employ; for it would grieve your hearts if, as I, you had seen so many miles together by goodly rivers uninhabited; and withal, to consider those parts of the world wherein you live to be even greatly burthened with abundance of people. These things I thought good to let you understand, being the truth of things as near as I could experimentally take knowledge of, and that you might on our behalf give God thanks, who hath dealt so favorably with us . . .

Your loving friend,

E.W.

Plymouth, in New England, this 11th of December, 1621.

The forerunner of our modern Thanksgiving was a harvest festival of feasting, spirited dancing, and games. This custom which the Pilgrims brought from England is reenacted annually at Plimoth Plantation, Massachusetts. Indians shared the first American celebration.

Evening settles on snow-becalmed Newark Village, isolated in the mountains of northeast Vermont.

Winter

We know it's coming, and yet it's always a surprise—that first cold snap of winter that paves a pond and invites us to stride across like the waterbugs did in June. On skates and skis and sleds we fly without leaving the ground, for once again winter has repealed the laws of locomotion.

And the laws of time as well. We watched for days as last spring's buds swelled and opened. We waited for weeks to pick the fruits of summer. And we raked for months as autumn played "she-loves-me-not" with the falling leaves. But winter works her magic overnight. Drawing night's black curtain long before our evening has begun, she spends the dark hours redecorating in ermine white. Sifting and drifting and dusting and crusting, snow is winter's invitation to bundle up and be a kid again.

Winter is nature asleep—and how beautifully she dreams! Snow in clean coverlets tucking in shivering mouse and sleepy chipmunk, snow in cresting drifts, snow costuming the trees and shrubs in absurd party hats and fanciful epaulets, snow shaped in sparkling sculptures that only yesterday were hydrants and the lawn chairs we forgot to put away last fall. An ice storm turns a patch of woods into a cathedral of glass, its traceried windows scattering rainbows on a polished floor.

"Merry Christmas" echoes from friend to friend on hard, clean air uncluttered with birdsong and insect rasp. "Happy New Year" bursts from an opened doorway to warm the partygoer even before he steps inside.

The sun is far to the south now. A tree that stored its energy for half a century warms a living room as its logs smolder on the hearth. Outside, the other trees know the sun will return, and they are ready, with buds on their twigs and sap in their roots. We speak of the promise of spring, but the trees tell us we are wrong. It is winter that promises. Spring delivers.

December

Dec. 1. Very bright and clear with a cold wind from the north east. For many weeks past the birds have been coming to be fed in the mornings. Today I put out a cocoa-nut,—to the great joy of the tom-tits, numbers of them were pecking away at it all through the day,—mostly Blue tits.

4. Three days of rain, wind and sunshine.

7. Hard white frost and fog. This is the first real winter's day we have had. Crowds of birds came to be fed this morning; There were great battles among the Tits over the cocoa-nut; and once a Robin got right into it, and refused to let the Tits approach, until he had had all he wanted. I don't think the Robins really care for cocoa-nut; but they don't like to see the Tits enjoying anything, without claiming a share.

9 We woke up to a storm of whirling snowflakes this morning,— the first snow this winter. The storm was soon over however and it was followed by bright sunshine and a sharp frost at night.

10. Cold, frosty day, It seems as if winter had begun in earnest; but the fore-casts prophecy a speedy change.

12 Wind and rain with bright intervals. There was a most beautiful rain-bow visible in the morning for about ten minutes.

14 Heavy fall of snow

20 After a rapid thaw and four days of wonderfully mild, still weather, without wind or rain; the wind has gone round to the east and it looks as if we might have a frosty Christmas after all.

25. We woke to a snowy Christmas morning; sunshine later and sharp frost at night.

26 Another heavy fall of snow in the night.

"Amid the leafless thorn
the merry Wren,
When icicles hang dripping
from the rock,
Pipes her perennial lay;
Even when the flakes
Broad on her pinions fall,
She lightly flies
Athwart the shower
and sings upon the wing."
                    James Graham.

Wren
(Sylvia troglodytes)
and
Hedge Sparrow
(Accentor modulares)

Now the Animal World Goes to Sleep

Its winter snooze broken by hunger pangs, a raccoon cautiously tests the nippy air before leaving to search for food. The masked rogue prowls on nights when the temperature is above 30°F. Food is of no concern to the hibernating brown bats and marmot. In autumn, they build up a life-sustaining layer of fat that lasts until spring. Little brown bats enter hibernation as late as November; the marmot is inactive for about two months.

To Thoreau it was "that grand old poem called winter," but neither writers nor the general public usually speak so well of it. Ski enthusiasts excepted, few exclaim "Winter has come!" in the tone of voice they reserve for the more popular seasons and Shelley couldn't think of anything more favorable to say than that spring could not be far behind.

Snow, ice, and bitter winds seem to fall upon the living world like some irretrievable calamity and to leave nothing but ruin where trees had rustled and flowers bloomed. Even those to whom the love of nature is a dominant passion sometimes speak of "the dead of winter" and a winter landscape can indeed look like a lunar one—as though forever silent and never to live again.

But of course "the dead of winter" is wrong. Even "sleep of winter" doesn't cover everything but it does cover a great deal more. Though a few of the animals such as the fox, the rabbit, and the winter birds are wide awake, most of them are, like most of the plants, more or less quiescent—some lying motionless but awake; some in the half-sleep of the bear whose young are born while their mother dozes; some in that deep sleep called hibernation; many more locked in the death-like suspension of all visible activity characteristic of the wintering egg, seed, chrysalis, or cocoon.

Even for the proudly technological human being, survival is to some extent a problem and there are few if any animals who do not either withdraw in one way or another from win-

ter or face an intensified struggle for existence. The chickadees who come in from the woods where they have summered and the juncos who come down from the north may sometimes seem positively to enjoy a good blizzard but they are cheerful rather than safe, for a rain followed by a hard freeze will take a heavy toll.

Obviously all the various devices by which winter is eluded or made endurable have been learned in the course of time. At least all the higher animals and plants must have got their start in regions where winter never came and, if the evolutionists are right, must have slowly worked out their astonishingly varied techniques for surviving gradually increasing rigors. What is true of the animals is true of the plants too—but

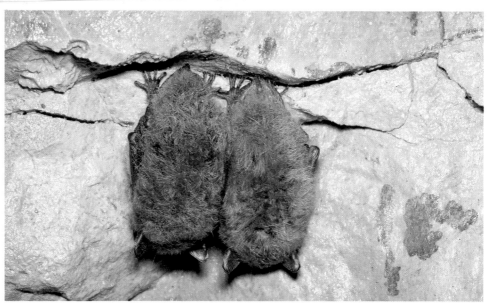

with differences. And if we leave the plants aside for the moment to consider only that half of animate creation with which we are closely allied, we may be humiliated to discover how little man himself has added to the techniques invented by his humble cousins. The great Promethean discovery that fire can be started and controlled is his alone. Otherwise he does only what other animals were doing many millennia before his appearance—building shelters, getting heavier clothing, storing food, or simply going to a region where it doesn't get too cold.

This last maneuver is called "taking a winter vacation" when men perform it and "migration" in animals. Many of the latter make minor shifts from a cooler spot to a warmer, but on any

large scale migration is practiced almost exclusively by the hoofed animals (like the caribou of the north) and, preeminently of course, by the birds. Some of them, the chickadee for instance, are found the year around in the same regions; others, like the robin, may move a short distance; many others, like the oriole and the tiny hummingbird, go all the way to Central or South America, while one frantic world traveler, the arctic tern, spends the northern summer in the arctic and the southern summer in the antarctic.

Why do they do it and how do they do it? No problem of animal behavior has been more discussed or still involves more mysteries. What is south for one bird is north for an-

other. In New England, for instance, your oriole moves out and your junco comes in. Many birds nest in the most northerly part of their range, principally perhaps because the summer days are longest there and afford more daylight hours in which to hunt food for the voracious young. Why can a chickadee stand a New England winter while an oriole cannot? At least this much may be said: it is not exclusively a matter of resistance to cold. The chickadee can find seeds, insect eggs, and scraps in winter; most of the flying-insect eaters must go where insects are active the year around. How do birds know when to take off? Experiments seem to prove pretty conclusively that the lengthening and shortening of daylight rather than any change in temperature is the

Snow sometimes makes hunting easier for predators that can't sleep winter away. The snowy owl squats unnoticed atop a drift to attack unwary lemming, hare, bird, or mouse. The mouse may hide in its tunnel under the snow only to be eaten by a weasel or by a coyote (below) who digs in after it. Pumas and wolves can prowl on crusted snow where deer and caribou break through, losers in winter's fateful lottery.

signal. How do they find their way? That is still largely a disputed question. As late as the eighteenth century an educated man could still believe that swallows spent the winter beneath the mud of pond bottoms. And what they do do is no less remarkable. Our chimney swifts spend winter in the Amazon basin. Why there? Well, perhaps only for the same reason that some human beings always vacation in the same spot. "Our family has been going there for years."

But what of the many kinds of animals which, like most human beings, cannot manage a winter vacation? Most of the mammals are active. Deer, weasels, rabbits, and wildcats store no food; they browse or hunt all winter. In the water under the ice muskrats find food, and the prudent squirrels and field mice lay up winter stores. The field mouse also supplements the store by foraging under the snow as he makes his way along the tunnels he digs through the snow. Gray squirrels too are equally active, though in really inclement weather they may remain for days curled up snugly in their leaf-houses high in some tree.

If all these animals as well as the wintering birds "can take it," why can't others not too distantly related? Why is it that the flying squirrel is active all winter while the eastern chipmunk retires in autumn to a well-stored burrow and stays there almost continuously, even, in colder climates, sinking into a more or less complete dormancy? And why do the wood-chucks and the brown bats fall into complete hibernation?

No animal habit is stranger, for hibernation is not the same as sleep, no matter how deep. It seems halfway to death and one wonders if it could have arisen first in animals which barely escaped death in the course of increasingly rigorous winters. Men on the point of freezing are said to grow drowsy and that is exactly what happens to the hibernators as the cold comes on. The process begins at about fifty degrees. They grow sleepier and sleepier and their body temperature drops because the success of the maneuver depends upon the fact that they cease to be "warm-blooded." Thus the temperature of a hibernating woodchuck may fall to about thirty-seven degrees; his rate of

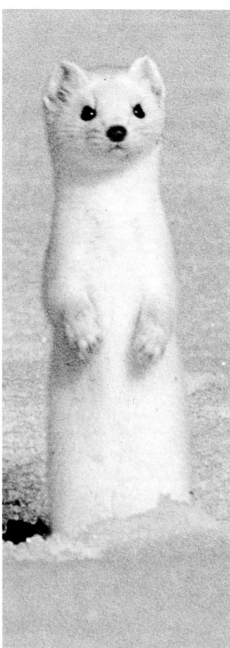

breathing declines from thirty times a minute to as little as once in five minutes. His heart may beat only four or five times per minute and he may remain completely motionless for days on end. Wakening is rapid. Metabolism which was very low rises to a fever pitch and before long the woodchuck is again as good as new.

It used to be said that no bird ever hibernates—perhaps because he knows the better trick of going south if necessary. But at least one bird does, namely a southwestern relative of the eastern whippoorwill who tucks himself into a cranny and stays there in the deep sleep of real hibernation. Truly a most unbirdlike habit.

Warm blood kept at a constant temperature by a sort of internal thermostat which opens the metabolic draft

when necessary is a characteristic of the mammals and birds alone. Its advantage is that it enables the animal to be as lively in cold weather as in warm whereas the cold-blooded reptiles and amphibians move and live at a variable rate which grows more sluggish as the temperature falls. The same is true of many insects and you may, if so inclined, tell the summer evening temperature by the green tree cricket, who chirps at a rate which a formula will translate into degrees Fahrenheit.

But warm-bloodedness has its disadvantages too. Cold can reach a point where the blood temperature cannot any longer be maintained and the animal will die unless he either migrates to a warmer place or, like the few hibernators, has learned the trick of

becoming temporarily a cold-blooded instead of a warm-blooded animal. For the normally cold-blooded it is all very much simpler. Expose a man or any warm-blooded animal continuously to a very low temperature and he will die. But a frog may be frozen in a cake of ice and come back to life when the ice thaws.

That is an extreme case but many of the humbler creatures who disappear from the scene in autumn or winter are simply somewhere out of sight sleeping the inclement season away. Of those insects who pass the winter in the adult stage, millions are tucked away in crannies, in or under the bark of trees, and millions more below the ground cover of dead leaves. To them a snow blanket is a great help; where the surface of the ground

The seemingly dead plants of winter mean life itself to many animals. The grizzly's last bedtime snack often includes pine needles and dry leaves. The beaver dines on tree branches retrieved from its stockpile on the pond bottom. Red squirrels dip into their private caches of up to a bushel of nuts and cones. Mule deer depend on plants and trees that outreach the deepening snow, the bison on grasses uncovered by its snow-plow head.

is nearly zero two inches of snow may keep the temperature a few inches below ground just a bit above freezing. Some frogs and toads pass the winter quiescent in the mud of pond bottoms, but the little spring peeper who will somewhat prematurely announce the end of winter around the middle of a New England March sleeps the worst of the weather away under the frozen leaves near the pond to which he will return to breed and sing as soon as a little relaxing of the winter's cold makes him active again.

"**N**ot dead but sleeping" is, then, the most fitting epitaph to write over the tomb of a winter landscape. But of course some do die in their sleep and there are other species to whom the end of summer is, for the

individual, always the end of the world. That is true of a great many, but by no means all, insects, some of which have come to the end of their life span and would not live very much longer even if kept artificially warm. The female lays her eggs and dies, much as an annual plant produces its seed before it withers and the seeds of plant and animal alike survive. Even more curious are the in-betweens, especially the moths and the butterflies, who are caterpillars first, then chrysalises or cocoons, and finally the beautifully winged insects. Perhaps just to show that there is more than one way of doing a thing some species winter as adults, some as eggs, and some in the cocoon where the caterpillar will be born again—and born better.

Most people probably know rather more about plants in winter than they do about animals. Even nongardeners are aware that some are annuals which would live for but one summer whether winter ever came or not and that others are perennial, some evergreen during the fiercest blizzards, others merely losing their leaves like many trees and shrubs, and still others retiring underground to a sort of hibernation in root or tuber.

Superficially these seem roughly analogous to the various methods adopted by animals but the reason why many plants must take some defensive measures is not the same. They are not warm-blooded or cold-blooded. They are, indeed, not blooded at all and while they have many different reactions to changes of tem-

perature the most obvious cause of death when freezing sets in is the simple fact that ice crystals forming inside the leaves penetrate like needles the living cells and so destroy them. Woody plants can meet that problem by sacrificing the leaves and exposing to the air only the dead covering of bark; herbaceous plants by dying down to the protected root. But why, then, can the evergreens keep their leaves; why do some that are not evergreen droop at the first breath of chill while the skunk cabbage often starts its growth in marshes still rimmed with ice? Two of the many answers to that are that winter-resistant leaves are tougher in texture and also that in winter many of them contain less water to freeze and expand. But the subject is so very com-

plicated that some readers will prefer to say merely "the nature of the beast" and let it go at that.

Perhaps the most striking difference between plant and animal adaptation to winter is that to far more plants than animals winter is not merely something to be endured but something which is absolutely necessary. A woodchuck kept awake in warm quarters all winter will not die because he did not get his accustomed sleep but many perennial plants must go into winter dormancy or they will die. Also, many seeds will not germinate and many buds formed in late summer or autumn will not unfold in spring unless they have been frozen. Bring the bare branches of forsythia into the house in autumn and the buds

will never open. Bring them in in January after they have been well frozen and they will—long before spring has come. Many of the animals active in winter deserve your pity. But don't pity the sleeping plants!

Winter is as good a time as spring to observe the ingenuity of nature and to marvel at the many different ways—sometimes one is tempted to say all the possible ways—in which a given problem is solved. Why have some plants and animals chosen one and some another? Evolution gives part of the answer when it stresses adaptation. But why, in a given instance, this adaptation rather than another? It can hardly be just to make the world more interesting. But at least that is exactly what it does do.

Joseph Wood Krutch

The Pond in Winter

Standing on the snow-covered plain, as if in a pasture amid the hills, I cut my way first through a foot of snow, and then a foot of ice, and open a window under my feet, where, kneeling to drink, I look down into the quiet parlor of the fishes, pervaded by a softened light as through a window of ground glass, with its bright sanded floor the same as in summer; there a perennial waveless serenity reigns as in the amber twilight sky, corresponding to the cool and even temperament of the inhabitants. Heaven is under our feet as well as over our heads.

Early in the morning, while all things are crisp with frost, men come with fishing-reels and slender lunch, and let down their fine lines through the snowy field to take pickerel and perch; wild men, who instinctively follow other fashions and trust other authorities than their townsmen, and by their goings and comings stitch towns together in parts where else they would be ripped. They sit and eat their luncheon in stout fear-naughts on the dry oak leaves on the shore, as wise in natural lore as the citizen is in artificial. They never consult with books, and know and can tell much less than they have done. The things which they practice are said not yet to be known. Here is one fishing for pickerel with grown perch for bait. You look into his pail with wonder as into a summer pond, as if he kept summer locked up at home, or knew where she had retreated. How, pray, did he get these in midwinter? Oh, he got worms out of rotten logs since the ground froze, and so he caught them. His life itself passes deeper in nature than the studies of the naturalist penetrate; himself a subject for the naturalist. The latter raises the moss and bark gently with his knife in search of insects; the former lays open logs to their core with his axe, and moss and bark fly far and wide. He gets his living by barking trees. Such a man has some right to fish, and I love to see nature carried out in him. The perch swallows the grub-worm, the pickerel swallows the perch, and the fisherman swallows the pickerel; and so all the chinks in the scale of being are filled.

Henry David Thoreau

O Come All Ye Bird Counters

The Audubon Christmas Bird Count is the longest-running, farthest-ranging, most popular, least-understood sporting event of the year. It's an annual exercise in mass masochism, regional chauvinism, and outerwear exhibitionism, but for thousands of birdwatchers, it's the Super Bowl, World Series, and Kentucky Derby all rolled into one.

In preparation for the biggest birding bash of the year, teams from the Aleutians to Newfoundland and from Hawaii to the Virgin Islands begin right after Thanksgiving to organize their game plans, polish their optical gear, and ready kayaks, marsh bug-

Cardinal

Taking December's blasts in stride, friends keep a cherished Christmas custom: counting birds that winter in their community. Within 7.5 miles of Estes Park, Colorado, they and others may tally 45 species before nightfall.

gies, fishing boats, air boats, airplanes, helicopters, bicycles, golf carts, cars, trucks, jeeps, and even the old-fashioned feet that will take them out to wherever the birds are at Christmas time.

Each year over 30,000 birdwatchers, from school children to octogenarians, take part in the Christmas count. Many old-timers boast forty, fifty, and sixty years of participation.

This epidemic winter madness started in 1900, when Frank M. Chapman, the ornithologist who edited the Audubon Society's *Bird Lore* magazine, suggested a substitute for the hunters' traditional Christmas-time massacre, the "side hunt." As Chapman wrote, "It is not many years ago that sportsmen were accustomed to meet on Christmas Day, 'choose sides,' and then . . . hie them to the fields and woods on the cheerful mission of killing practically everything in fur and feathers that crossed their path. We hope that all our readers who have the opportunity will aid us in making

[the new bloodless sport] a success by spending a portion of their Christmas Day with the birds and sending us a report of their 'hunt' before they retire that night."

That first year twenty-six persons in twenty-five groups responded to Chapman's challenge. The longest list reported was from Pacific Grove, California: thirty-six species. Chapman himself took second place, reporting eighteen species from Englewood, New Jersey.

It was not exactly an auspicious beginning, but the madness spread. By 1977 the number of counting groups (known as counts) had reached 1,247. In almost every year since 1900, totals of counts, observers, species, and number of birds seen have risen. In addition, the rules have gradually been formalized. Each group is now confined to a search area with a fifteen-mile diameter, and the search is restricted to any one calendar day within a two-week period centered on Christmas. Methods of reporting have been standardized to give more scientific value.

The people who happily give up a part of their Christmas holidays, or Christmas itself, and pay a $1.50 participation fee for the privilege of slogging through mud and sand, or of plodding through rain or snow, or of risking their necks on mountain peaks to count wild birds are not all crazy—despite appearances. Some are scientists, conservationists, and major museum officials.

The mass of Christmas bird counters, however, are dedicated amateurs—school teachers (lots of them), taxi drivers, housewives, writers, farmers, airline pilots, bankers, school children, and military servicemen. More men take part than women, although birding is still looked upon in some circles as an effete pastime.

This is nonsense, of course. Birding can be far more taxing than many true "sports." Men and women often spend all day on foot, walking ten miles through fields and wasteland. Some brave 20-below temperatures while others climb to summits through rain and sleet, often for meager rewards in bird sightings.

At the other extreme are those people along our southern and California coastlines who enjoy balmy weather and concentrations of a great variety of birds. Of the teams that regularly manage to find more than 150 species in their respective areas, more than two-thirds are from California, Florida, and Texas.

I well remember my own first Christmas count. The date was December 26, 1930, and I was a member of an all-boy bird club at my school in suburban Long Island. Nine of us were out that gray, rain-spattered day—on foot, on bicycles, or crammed into our science teacher's rattling Chevrolet—to scour the marshes, bays, and woodlands of our area. We were up before dawn and out until after dark. When we gathered at our teacher's house to tally the results, we had identified a grand total of forty-eight species! That, as it turned out, was the lowest number we ever recorded. In 1976 fifty-nine of us found 122 species in that same southern Nassau County area, and the forty-two year cumulative total is now 200 species—remarkable for an area at that latitude in late December.

Christmas counting means more to most of us than merely a day in the field. Some of the pleasure is the companionship of old friends as we plough through the brambles by day and meet for the ceremonial din-

ner after dark. Following dinner, the compiler calls the roll of species, with each party leader giving his group's total, and a final tally is made.

The southern Nassau count is rather informal in organization as compared with such superpowers as Cocoa, Florida, and Freeport, Texas. In Freeport, Victor Emanuel musters an army of close to one hundred for a meticulously planned campaign. Advance parties scour the terrain for days in advance, "staking out" the rarities so that they can be easily

Snowy egret

chalked up on counting day. Walkie-talkie radios provide communication; dogs are used to flush game and marsh birds; and tape recorders carrying the calls of secretive species are used to lure the choice varieties, such as rails and owls, a practice that is increasingly frowned upon as harassment of the birds.

The strategy pays off year after year for Victor Emanuel: in 1972 his Freeport count set a new world's record of 226 species, a fantastic number of different birds to find in winter in one small circle of land and water. In 1976 they found only 196 species, but it was the top count in the United States, closely followed by Corpus Christi, Texas, whose 24 observers saw 195, and the Point Reyes Peninsula, California team with 193.

Apart from the physical pleasure of the day afield, the spiritual pleasure of the companionship, the intrigue of the hunt, and the fierce competition, the Christmas count yields information of considerable scientific value. By locating our wintering species and estimating their numbers, we can discern where certain species are increasing or declining. We can determine the areas of greatest abundance for each species and try to determine the reason. We still don't know why Cincinnati always lists more cardinals than any other area in the country.

In 1976, of 74 million birds counted, 80 percent were starlings, blackbirds, and house sparrows. The single most abundant species was the red-winged blackbird, which numbered 21 million. The counts also give us firmer figures on some of our rarest species.

Obviously, the mass of information gathered is of little use unless it is critically edited and published somewhere. That somewhere is the July issue of the National Audubon Society's magazine for birdwatchers, *American Birds*.

Where it will all end is anybody's guess. Since Canada, middle and northern South America, and the Caribbean have been admitted and groups from other countries are joining the campaign, there seems to be nothing to bar a 2,000-count or even 3,000-count Christmas. When that day comes, new and perhaps computerized methods of handling the information will have to be devised. We are already planning for such a deluge, determined not to let success kill our crazy Christmas carnival.

Robert Arbib

Goldfinch

A Christmas Tree for the Birds

A Christmas tree for the birds can be as simple or as elaborate as you care to make it. The one shown opposite is an example of how decorative such a tree can be. Situated in the front yard or on the patio, it can add beauty and excitement to your home as well as provide a banquet that will last the birds through the twelve days of Christmas. After the food has been eaten, the birds will use the tree as shelter. Many conifers, such as the balsam, hold needles well into the spring, protecting the birds during the coldest months of the year.

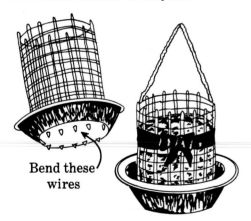

Bend these wires

Bird Feeder
Materials:
4″ aluminum foil pan
½″ mesh hardware cloth, 8½″ x 4″
red paint
12″ red pipe cleaner
12″ piece of red ribbon

Directions:
1. Make a cylinder of the hardware cloth. Place cylinder in foil pan and push ends of wire through bottom. Bend wires on underside of pan to hold basket in place.

2. Paint feeder bright red. Run a red ribbon around the hardware cloth at center. Attach red pipe cleaner for handle.
3. Fill the basket with suet and place grain in pan. (Grind suet first, then melt and cut into cubes.)

Popcorn Strings
With heavy-duty thread, string popcorn in 24″ lengths and hang vertically in 12″ loops. Wire to tree.

Pine Cones
Twist florist wire around pine cone and fasten, leaving a length for hanging. Spread peanut butter on cone.

Treetop Ornament
Materials:
6″ styrofoam ball
stalks of millet and sorghum
green gumdrops, leaf-shaped
peanuts in shell
heavy wire or pieces of coat hanger
3′ dowel, ½″ diameter
small florist's picks

Directions:
1. Mount the styrofoam on the 3′ dowel, adding glue around dowel.
2. Push wire through peanut shells, using 8 to 12 peanuts. Use as many wires as desired; they may also vary in length. Glue around the wire where it goes into the ball.
3. Force stalks of millet and sorghum into styrofoam ball.
4. Use florist's picks to cover surface of ball with green gumdrops.
5. Wire the dowel to the leader of the tree so that the ornament is centered on the treetop.

Orange Basket
Make three holes equidistant around the edge of half an orange shell. Push ends of a 12″ pipe cleaner through two of the holes; push the end of another pipe cleaner through third hole and twist it around the center of first pipe cleaner. Leave the remaining 6″ for hanger. Fill with nut meats and cranberries.

Marshmallow Stick
String six marshmallows on small-sized wire. Tie a bow of red ribbon at bottom and hang vertically on tree.

Doughnuts
Decorate doughnut with a sprig of red-berried holly. Loop a red ribbon through hole in doughnut; hang to tree by wire.

Cranberry Rings
String cranberries on 6″ lengths of wire strong enough to hold a shape. Curve each cranberry-laden wire into a 4″ ring, leaving 2″ of wire for hanging.

Recipes for the Birds

What a treat your bird friends will have this winter if you will stir up some of their favorite dishes! These recipes are fun to make and will delight the guests at your backyard feeders. They will also provide the extra warmth and energy birds need at this time of year. Remember that birds wake up and go to sleep at much the same time each day—usually with the sun. So check and refill your bird-feeders early each morning and again before it gets dark. Once you start feeding, keep it up until the tree leaves are out in spring. Then there will be plenty of insects and other natural food around again.

Irene Cosgrove

ABOUT THE INGREDIENTS

Raw Beef Suet: Suet is very important in providing energy and warmth during the cold winter months. In preparing suet, always put it through a meat grinder before melting it down. It makes a smoother liquid. Reheat to make a solid suet cake. Ask your Mom or Dad to help you with this.

Sand: Birds need to eat a gritty substance like sand to grind and digest the coarse foods they eat. Ordinary beach or sandbox sand will do, or you can buy commercial bird gravel for this purpose.

Kitchen scraps: Store leftover cake, doughnuts, cookies and pie crust in a covered plastic container. Keep crusts and stale bread in another.

Seeds and Grains: Sunflower seeds, cracked corn, peanut hearts or pieces, and wild birdseed can be bought at your local feed or hardware shop.

Flicker Fricassee

1 cup Grape Nuts	1 cup peanut hearts
1 cup raisins	or pieces
¼ teaspoon sand	1 1/3 cups raw suet

Into an 8″ x 8″ cake pan, put Grape Nuts, raisins, sand and peanut hearts or pieces. Set aside. Put suet through a meat grinder, melt down in a double boiler and set aside to cool and harden slightly. Reheat and pour suet over dry ingredients. Refrigerate until firm, cut in pieces and serve in plastic coated wire basket on tree trunk.

Nuthatch Nibble

1½ cups raw suet	1 cup sunflower seeds
2 cups bread crumbs	1 teaspoon sand
1 cup popped popcorn	

Combine popcorn, bread crumbs and sunflower seeds in medium size bowl and set aside. After putting suet through meat grinder, melt it down in a double boiler. Remove from heat and allow to harden slightly. Reheat and while in liquid form pour suet over dry ingredients. Sprinkle with sand. Stir mixture with a fork until well coated. Turn out onto wax paper. Bring paper up around suet, pressing to form a ball. Refrigerate until firm. Remove wax paper and place in netted suet bag.

Jay Jambalaya

1½ cups raw suet	½ cup bread crumbs
¼ cup meat scraps	1 cup peanut hearts or
1 cup cornmeal	pieces
	1 teaspoon sand

Do not remove fat from meat scraps; put them through meat grinder and place in a medium size bowl. To this add cornmeal, bread crumbs, peanut hearts or pieces, and sand for grit. Cut up suet and put through meat grinder. Place in double boiler, melt, set aside to cool and harden. Reheat and while in liquid form pour suet over dry ingredients. Spoon into suet container or feeder. Refrigerate until firm.

Grosbeak Goulash

½ cup sunflower seeds	¼ cup All-bran
½ cup hamster pellets	¼ teaspoon sand
1/3 cup dog biscuits	¾ cup suet

Put sunflower seeds, hamster pellets, crushed dog biscuits, All-bran and sand into a coconut shell half. Set aside. Put suet through meat grinder and place in double boiler. Melt and set aside to cool and harden slightly. Reheat and while in liquid form pour suet over ingredients in coconut shell. Refrigerate to harden.

Waxwing Wedge

1½ cups raw suet	¾ cup raisins
1 large apple	1 teaspoon sand
2 cups kitchen scraps	

Peel and core apple. Put peel through meat grinder and cut apple into small cubes. Place in 8″ x 8″ cake pan or foil container. Add kitchen scraps and raisins that have been steamed in a little water until plump. Mix well. Put suet through grinder, then melt down in a double boiler. Set aside to cool and harden slightly. Reheat and while in liquid form, pour suet over fruit and scraps combination. Add sand. Refrigerate until firm. Cut into wedges to fit your suet feeder.

Christmas Trees

*This 1916 poem by Robert Frost (1874-1963)
evokes his earlier years as a Vermont farmer.
Drawing his symbols from common experience,
he became one of America's best loved poets.*

The city had withdrawn into itself
And left at last the country to the country;
When between whirls of snow not come to lie
And whirls of foliage not yet laid, there drove
A stranger to our yard, who looked the city,
Yet did in country fashion in that there
He sat and waited till he drew us out,
A-buttoning coats, to ask him who he was.
He proved to be the city come again
To look for something it had left behind
And could not do without and keep its Christmas.
He asked if I would sell my Christmas trees;
My woods—the young fir balsams like a place
Where houses all are churches and have spires.
I hadn't thought of them as Christmas trees.
I doubt if I was tempted for a moment
To sell them off their feet to go in cars
And leave the slope behind the house all bare,
Where the sun shines now no warmer than the moon.
I'd hate to have them know it if I was.
Yet more I'd hate to hold my trees, except
As others hold theirs or refuse for them,
Beyond the time of profitable growth—
The trial by market everything must come to.
I dallied so much with the thought of selling.
Then whether from mistaken courtesy
And fear of seeming short of speech, or whether
From hope of hearing good of what was mine,
I said, "There aren't enough to be worth while."

"I could soon tell how many they would cut,
You let me look them over."

                              "You could look.
But don't expect I'm going to let you have them."

Pasture they spring in, some in clumps too close
That lop each other of boughs, but not a few
Quite solitary and having equal boughs
All round and round. The latter he nodded "Yes" to,
And paused to say beneath some lovelier one,
With a buyer's moderation, "That would do."
I thought so too, but wasn't there to say so.
He climbed the pasture on the south, crossed over,
and came down on the north.

                              He said, "A thousand."

"A thousand Christmas trees!—at what apiece?"

He felt some need of softening that to me:
"A thousand trees would come to thirty dollars."

Then I was certain I had never meant
To let him have them. Never show surprise!
But thirty dollars seemed so small beside
The extent of pasture I should strip, three cents
(For that was all they figured out apiece)—
Three cents so small beside the dollar friends
I should be writing to within the hour
Would pay in cities for good trees like those,
Regular vestry-trees whole Sunday Schools
Could hang enough on to pick off enough.

A thousand Christmas trees I didn't know I had!
Worth three cents more to give away than sell,
As may be shown by a simple calculation.
Too bad I couldn't lay one in a letter.
I can't help wishing I could send you one
In wishing you herewith a Merry Christmas.

Robert Frost

The Plants of Christmas

English Holly
Ilex aquifolium

Holly was known and revered by early British Druids
and Roman pagans. The Druids thought it was
a special favorite of the sun because it was evergreen.
The Romans used it as a charm to ward off
lightning and evil spells
and believed its blossoms could repel poison.
They sent sprigs of holly to their friends
during Saturnalia. The early Christian Church forbade
the use of holly, particularly during the Saturnalia,
but the Romans largely ignored the ban.
So did the British, among whom arose the custom
of hanging sprigs of holly about the house
as hiding places for Christmas elves and fairies.
In Germany a soberer legend evolved
about the holly, which was called Christdorn,
or Christ's crown of thorns.
The berries were believed to have been white
until they were stained by Christ's blood.

Ivy
Hedera helix

The traditions held holly to be a man's plant,
ivy a woman's. To the Greeks, ivy was an emblem
of happiness, fertility, and honor.
Poets were crowned with it.
Bacchus, the god of wine, wore a
rather rakish crown of ivy, perhaps because
it was supposed to prevent intoxication.
Also an emblem of fidelity,
it was used in wreaths for the newly married.
Its black berries at one time were thought to be
a remedy for the plague. They weren't, of course.
Ivy was used as decoration for churches and homes
at Christmas, but only for outer passages
and on doorways, where it was put up
on Christmas Eve, taken down on Candlemas Eve.
And poles twined with ivy and holly,
the woman's plant and the man's, were set up
for Christmas sports and games.

Poinsettia
Euphorbia pulcherrima

The poinsettia, native to the New World,
is one of the very few strictly American plants
that have been absorbed
into the body of Christmas legends.
It has become a traditional Christmas plant
chiefly because of its bright red color.
But there is a Mexican legend about the poinsettia
that clearly is a lineal descendant of the legend about
hellebore, the Christmas rose.
In this Mexican version, a little girl,
child of a family of poor peons, was on her way to church
on Christmas eve and was so sad
at having no gift to place at the altar
for the Virgin and Child that she wept.
An angel heard and told her to gather
an armload of twigs from the roadside.
She did, and by the time she reached the church
they were in full bloom, an armload of poinsettias,
a beautiful gift to place at the altar.

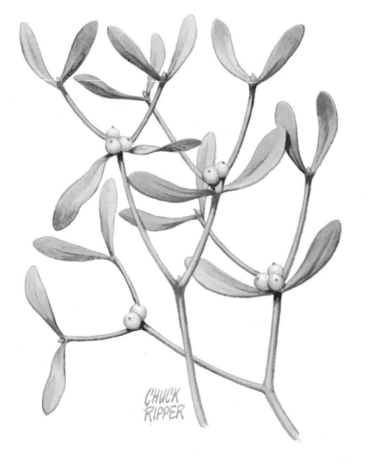

European Mistletoe
Viscum album

Mistletoe legends reach back to Norse mythology
and Virgil's *Aeneid*. Mistletoe was the
Druids' golden herb.
Robed in white, they cut it with a golden sickle
and caught it in a white cloth
before it touched the ground.
It symbolized purity and strength,
was hung in houses to bring happiness,
promote romance, enforce peace. If enemies
met beneath the mistletoe they disarmed and kept
truce that day. Because of the plant's pagan associations,
the Church banned it from Christmas ceremonies,
but its magic was so strong that people
used it secretly and even
monks wore it as a hidden amulet.
It was believed to exorcise witches and demons,
protect from fits, lung fever, tremors, and poison.
European mistletoe grows on oaks.
American mistletoe grows on maples and tupelos.

Hal Borland

Decorate Your Tree the Natural Way

S omehow, our old log cabin snugged in a cove of the Blue Ridge Mountains did not seem the place for a tinselled, glittery Christmas tree. The tree should be simple, "natural-like," as the mountain people would say.

I bent a scrap of old chicken wire into a cone "tree" about 30 inches high and poked in sprigs of fir and boxwood and then roamed the woods and fields nearby to choose from nature's bountiful supply of decorating materials.

Back home I emptied my collecting bag onto a table along with glue, florist's wire, tape, and calico and felt scraps and let my imagination run wild. Acorn cups became candle holders trimmed with dogwood berries, and jimson pods held other berries. Tiny felt cones were stuffed with reindeer lichen or goldenrod fluff. Baskets woven from corn husks and felt soon bulged with hemlock cones, and other cones were snipped to make "flowers" and set on discs of calico or felt or muslin. Burdock burrs around felt discs became miniature wreaths and hickory hulls little boats cargoed with heaps of berries. Milkweed pods were so perfect in themselves that I used them unadorned.

The humble, unglittery Christmas tree won awards in a flower show. But the real joys for me were my outdoor ramble, completely "lost" in the natural world instead of in city crowds, and the satisfaction of sharing with others a way to deck our homes at Christmas with nature's free and renewable gifts.

Barbara Hallowell

Christmas Critters

Wouldn't it be jolly to have a leopard under your Christmas tree this year, crouching among the other packages? Or a little mouse peeking out from under the branches? It's easy to transform your Christmas-present boxes into these colorful critters. All you need are lots of brightly colored paper, some yarn, scissors, glue and a few odds and ends such as a styrofoam ball for a penguin's head. The critters here are only a few of those you can make. How many can you dream up yourself?

Delicious Holiday Wreaths

Orange Coffee Braid

5 to 5½ cups flour
½ cup sugar
1 teaspoon salt
2 packs active dry yeast
½ cup milk
½ cup water
½ cup butter or margarine
3 eggs
2 tablespoons grated orange rind
vegetable oil
1 tablespoon water

In large bowl, mix 2 cups of the flour with sugar, salt, and yeast. Combine milk, water, and butter in a saucepan; stir over low heat until mixture is very warm (not hot) to the touch. Gradually add this to flour mixture and beat at medium speed for 2 minutes. Add 2 eggs and 1 more cup flour; beat at high speed for 2 minutes. Work in orange rind and enough remaining flour to make a soft dough (about 1½ cups). On a well-floured board, pat dough out 1 inch thick and knead until dough is smooth and elastic, about 5 to 10 minutes. Shape dough into a ball and place in an oiled bowl, turning to grease top. Cover with a towel and put in a warm, draft-free place.

Let rise until doubled in bulk, about 1 hour. Punch dough down, knead a few times, and let rise again until doubled, about 45 minutes. Punch down once more, knead about a minute until smooth and elastic again.

Divide into 3 equal pieces. On a lightly floured tabletop, roll each piece into a strip 28 inches long, using palms of hands. Press the strips together at one end and interlace to form a braid. Shape braid into a ring on a greased baking sheet. Press overlapping ends together to close ring. Brush lightly with oil and let rise until doubled, about 30 minutes. Bake at 375° for 20 minutes. While it bakes, beat remaining egg with 1 tablespoon water.

When bread has baked 20 minutes, brush lightly with egg mixture. Bake 5 minutes more, brush again, and bake until bread is golden brown and sounds hollow when tapped with fingers (about 5 minutes more). Remove from baking sheet and cool on wire rack. Decorate with marzipan leaves and berries (recipe below). If you like, tie a ribbon bow at joined ends of braid. To serve: Cut in thin slices and serve with butter. To use as decoration only: Brush with several coats of varnish.

4 ounces almond paste
1 tablespoon light corn syrup
½ cup confectioners' sugar
red and green food coloring

To make marzipan holly, break up almond paste in a small bowl. Work in corn syrup until smooth; then, with your hand, work in confectioners' sugar. Mixture should be stiff and smooth. Break off about 1 tablespoon and color it red; color the remainder green. Shape the red part into berries. Flatten the green part on a sheet of plastic wrap and roll out very thin with a rolling pin. With a small sharp knife, cut out leaves. Use tip of knife to raise end of leaf; pick up leaf and arrange on wreath.

Sugarplum Cookies

2 cups blanched almonds
3 cups sifted flour
2 teaspoons vanilla
1 teaspoon rum extract
whole cloves
½ teaspoon salt
2 teaspoons baking powder
2/3 cup soft butter
1½ cups sugar
2 eggs
green pipe cleaners
assorted food coloring
assorted sugar crystals
chocolate sprinkles

Place almonds in blender and whir until finely grated. Sift together flour, salt, and baking powder. Stir in almonds. In a large bowl, beat butter until fluffy. Gradually beat in sugar, eggs, vanilla, and rum extract. Beat until light and fluffy. Stir in flour mixture. Blend well.

Form into a variety of fruit shapes, keeping each one fairly flat (½ inch high at thickest part) so all will bake evenly. Use whole clove, pod end in, for stems of pears and apples. Use pod, end out, for stems of lemons, limes, and oranges. Add pieces of pipe cleaner to cherries and strawberries. Place on greased cookie sheets. Bake at 350°F. for 5 to 8 minutes (when bottoms are golden, cookies are done). Cool on wire rack. Yield: about 60 cookies.

To make frosting, beat 2 egg whites until frothy. Beat in 2 cups confectioners' sugar. Divide frosting into small dishes—as many as the number of colors you'll want for your fruit. Use a small paintbrush to frost cookies, painting and sprinkling one at a time so sprinkles will stick.

Apples: Paint with red frosting, and sprinkle all over with red crystals.

Cherries: Paint red and sprinkle with red crystals.

Strawberries: Use light red frosting and red crystals.

Watermelon slices: Paint a rim of dark green and sprinkle with green crystals. Let dry. Paint rest pinkish-red; add red crystals, and chocolate sprinkles for seeds.

Lemons: Paint bright yellow; sprinkle with yellow or green crystals.

Bananas: Paint bright yellow; sprinkle with yellow or green crystals; add flecks of brown by pressing on chocolate sprinkles.

Grapes: Add a drop of green to yellow frosting; use green sprinkles.

Pears: Use yellow frosting; sprinkle with yellow; add red sprinkles for the blushing cheek.

Limes: Use green with a drop of yellow in it and yellow or green sprinkles.

Oranges: Mix yellow and red coloring to make orange frosting; sprinkle with yellow crystals.

To assemble wreath: Use straight pins to attach holly leaves to a 12-inch styrofoam ring. Next, press one toothpick at a time into ring leaving nearly ½ inch protruding on which to anchor each cookie; gently press the back of the cookie onto the pick. Space cookies with an eye for design. Takes 2 to 3 dozen assorted cookies.

The Father Christmas Letters

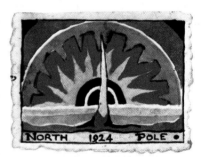

To the children of J.R.R. Tolkien, the interest and importance of Father Christmas extended beyond his filling of their stockings on Christmas Eve; for he wrote a letter to them every year, in which he described in words and pictures his house, and his friends, and the events, hilarious or alarming, at the North Pole. The first of the letters came in 1920, when John, the eldest, was three years old; and for over twenty years, through the childhoods of the three other children, Michael, Christopher and Priscilla, they continued to arrive each Christmas. Sometimes the envelopes, dusted with snow and bearing Polar postage stamps, were found in the house on the morning after his visit; sometimes the postman brought them; and letters that the children wrote themselves vanished from the fireplace when no one was about.

In the 1932 Christmas letter Father Christmas wrote about North Polar Bear, his chief assistant and chief cause of disasters, and how they met an attack by goblins against the cellars where the presents are stored until Christmas Eve.

1932

There have been lots of adventures you will want to hear about. It all began with the funny noises underground which started in the summer and got worse and worse. I was afraid an earthquake might happen. The North Polar Bear says he suspected what was wrong from the beginning. I only wish he had said something to me; and anyway it can't be quite true, as he was fast asleep when it began, and did not wake up till about Michael's birthday. However, he went off for a walk one day, at the end of November, I think, and never came back! About a fortnight ago I began to be really worried, for after all the dear old thing is really a lot of help, in spite of accidents, and very amusing.

One Friday evening (December 9th), there was a bumping at the front door and a snuffling. I thought he had come back, and lost his key (as often before); but when I opened the door there was another old bear there, a very fat and funny-shaped one. Actually it was the eldest of the remaining Cave-bears. (I had not seen him for centuries.)

'Do you want your North Polar Bear?' he said. 'If you do, you had better come and get him!'

It turned out he was lost in the caves (belonging to Cave-Bear, or so he says) not far from the ruins of my old house. He says he found a hole in the side of a hill and went inside because it was snowing. He slipped down a long slope, and lots of rock fell after him, and he found he could not climb up or get out again. But almost at once he smelt GOBLIN! and became interested and started to explore. Not very wise, for of course Goblins can't hurt him, but their caves are very dangerous. Naturally he soon got quite lost, and the Goblins shut off all their lights, and made queer noises and false echoes.

Goblins are to us very much what rats are to you, only worse, because they are very clever, and only better because there are, in these parts, very few. We thought there were none left. Long ago we had great trouble with them, that was about 1453, I believe, but we got the help of the Gnomes, who are their greatest enemies, and cleared them out. Anyway, there was poor old Polar Bear lost in the dark all among them, and alone until he met Cave-Bear, who lives there. Cave-Bear can see pretty well in the dark, and he offered to take Polar Bear to his private back door. So they set off together, but the Goblins were very excited and angry (Polar Bear had boxed one or two flat that came and poked him in the dark, and had said some very nasty things to them all), and they enticed him away by imitating Cave-Bear's voice, which of course they know very well. So Polar Bear got into a frightful dark part, all full of different passages, and he lost Cave-Bear, and Cave-Bear lost him.

'Light is what we need,' said Cave-Bear to me. So I got some of my special sparkling torches— which I sometimes use in my deepest cellars—and we set off that night. The caves are wonderful. I knew they were there, but not how many or how big they were. Of course the Goblins went off into the deepest holes and corners, and we soon found Polar Bear. He was getting quite long and thin with hunger, as he had been in the caves about a fortnight. He said, 'I should soon have been able to squeeze through a Goblin crack.'

Polar Bear himself was astonished when I brought light; for the most remarkable thing is that the walls of these caves are all covered with pictures, cut into the rock or painted on in red and brown and black. Some of them are very good (mostly of animals) and some are queer, and some bad, and there are many strange marks, signs and scribbles, some of which have a nasty look, and I am sure have something to do with black magic. Cave-Bear says these caves belong to him, and have belonged to him or his family since the days of his great-great-great-great-great-great-great-great-great-(multiplied by ten) grandfather; and the bears first had the idea of decorating the walls, and used to scratch pictures on them in soft parts—it was useful for sharpening the claws.

Then MEN came along—imagine it! Cave-Bear says there were lots about at one time, long ago, when the North Pole was somewhere else. (That was long before my time, and I have never heard old Grandfather Yule mention it, even, so I don't know if he's talking nonsense or not.) Many of the pictures were done by these Cave-men—the best ones, especially the big ones (almost life-size) of animals, some of which have since disappeared: there are dragons and quite a lot of mammoths. Men also put some of the black marks and pictures there, but the Goblins have scribbled all over the place. They can't draw well, and anyway they like nasty queer shapes best.

I have copied a whole page from the wall of the chief central cave. It is not, perhaps, quite as well drawn as the originals (which are very much larger) except the Goblin parts, which are easy. At the bottom of the page you will see a whole row of Goblin pictures—they must be very old, because the Goblin fighters are sitting on drasils: a very queer sort of dwarf 'dachshund' horse creature they used to use, but they have died out long ago. I believe the Red Gnomes finished them off, somewhere about Edward the Fourth's time. You will see some more on the pillar in my picture of the caves.

Doesn't the hairy rhinoceros look wicked? There is also a nasty look in the mammoth's eyes. You will also see an ox, a stag, a boar, a cave-bear (portrait of our Cave-Bear's seventy-first ancestor, he says) and some other kind of polarish but not quite polar bear. North Polar Bear would like to believe it is a portrait of one of his ancestors. Just under the bears you can see what is the best a Goblin can do at drawing reindeer!!!

But when I rescued Polar Bear we hadn't finished the adventures. At the beginning of last week we went into the cellars to get the stuff for England.

I said to Polar Bear, 'Somebody has been disarranging things here!'

Then last Saturday we went down and found nearly everything had disappeared out of the main cellar! Imagine my state of mind! Nothing hardly to send to anybody, and too little time to get or make enough new stuff.

Polar Bear said, 'I smell Goblin strong.' Eventually we found a large hole (but not big enough for us) leading to a tunnel, behind some packingcases in the West Cellar. As you will expect, we rushed off to find Cave-Bear and we went back to the caves. We soon understood the queer noises. It was plain the Goblins long ago had burrowed a tunnel from the caves to my old home (which was not so far from the end of their hills) and had stolen a good many things. We found some things more than a hundred years old, even a few parcels still addressed to your great-grand-people! But they had been very clever, and not too greedy, and I had not found out. Ever since I moved they must have been busy burrowing all the way to my cliff, boring, banging and blasting (as quietly as they could). At last they had reached my new cellars, and the sight of all the toys together was too much for them: they took all they could.

But I sent my patent green luminous smoke down the tunnel, and Polar Bear blew and blew it with our enormous kitchen bellows. They simply shrieked and rushed out the other (cave) end. But there were Red Gnomes there. I had specially sent for them—a few of the real old families are still in Norway. They captured hundreds of Goblins, and chased many more out into the snow (which they hate). We made them show us where they had hidden things, or bring them all back again, and by Monday we had got practically everything back. The Gnomes are still dealing with the Goblins, and promise there won't be one left by New Year—but I am not so sure—they will crop us again in a century or so, I expect.

J.R.R.Tolkien

My First Christmas Tree

I will begin by saying that we never had a Christmas tree in our house in the Wisconsin coulee; indeed, my father never saw one in a family circle till he saw that which I set up for my own children last year. But we celebrated Christmas in those days, always, and I cannot remember a time when we did not all hang up our stockings for "Sandy Claws" to fill. As I look back upon those days it seems as if the snows were always deep, the night skies crystal clear, and the stars especially lustrous with frosty sparkles of blue and yellow fire—and probably this was so, for we lived in a northern land where winter was usually stern and always long.

I recall one Christmas when "Sandy" brought me a sled, and a horse that stood on rollers—a wonderful tin horse which I very shortly split in two in order to see what his insides were. Father traded a cord of wood for the sled, and the horse cost twenty cents—but they made the day wonderful.

Another notable Christmas Day, as I stood in our front yard, midleg-deep in snow, a neighbor drove by closely muffled in furs, while behind his seat his son, a lad of twelve or fifteen, stood beside a barrel of apples, and as he passed he hurled a glorious big red one at me. It missed me, but bored a deep, round hole in the soft snow. I thrill yet with the remembered joy of burrowing for that delicious bomb. Nothing will ever smell quite as good as that Winesap or Northern Spy or whatever it was. It was a wayward impulse on the part of the boy in the sleigh, but it warms my heart after more than forty years.

We had no chimney in our home, but the stocking-hanging was a ceremony nevertheless. My parents, and especially my mother, entered into it with the best of humor. They always put up their own stockings or permitted us to do it for them—and they always laughed next morning when they found potatoes or ears of corn in them. I can see now that my mother's laugh had a tear in it, for she loved pretty things and seldom got any during the years that we lived in the coulee.

When I was ten years old we moved to Mitchell County, an Iowa prairie land, and there we prospered in such wise that our stockings always held toys of some sort, and even my mother's stocking occasionally sagged with a simple piece of jewelry or a new comb or brush. But the thought of a family tree remained the luxury of rich city dwellers; indeed it was not till my fifteenth or sixteenth year that our Sunday school rose to the extravagance of a tree, and it is of this wondrous festival that I write.

The land about us was only partly cultivated at this time, and our district schoolhouse, a bare little box, was set bleakly on the prairie; but the Burr Oak schoolhouse was not only larger, but it stood beneath great oaks as well and possessed the charm of a forest background through which a stream ran silently. It was our chief social center. There on a Sunday a regular preacher held "Divine service" with Sunday school as a sequence. On Friday nights the young people met in "ly-ceums," as we called them, to debate great questions or to "speak pieces" and read essays; and here it was that I saw my first Christmas tree.

I walked to that tree across four miles of moonlit snow. Snow? No, it was a floor of diamonds, a magical world, so beautiful that my heart still aches with the wonder of it and with the regret that it has

all gone—gone with the keen eyes and the bounding pulses of the boy.

Our home at this time was a small frame house on the prairie almost directly west of the Burr Oak grove, and as it was too cold to take the horses out my brother and I, with our tall boots, our visored caps and our long woolen mufflers, started forth afoot defiant of the cold. We left the gate on the trot, bound for a sight of the glittering unknown. The snow was deep and we moved side by side in the grooves made by the hoofs of the horses, setting our feet in the shine left by the broad shoes of the wood sleighs whose going had smoothed the way for us. Our breaths rose like smoke in the still air. It must have been ten below zero, but that did not trouble us in those days, and at last we came in sight of the lights, in sound of the singing, the laughter, the bells of the feast.

It was a poor little building without tower or bell and its low walls had but three windows on a side, and yet it seemed very imposing to me that night as I crossed the threshold and faced the strange people who packed it to the door. I say "strange people," for though I had seen most of them many times they all seemed somehow alien to me that night. I was an irregular attendant at Sunday school and did not expect a present, therefore I stood against the wall and gazed with open-eyed marveling at the shining pine which stood where the pulpit was wont to be. I was made to feel embarrassed by reason of the remark of a boy who accused me of having forgotten to comb my hair.

This was not true, but the cap I wore always matted my hair down over my brow, and then, when I lifted it off, invariably disarranged it completely. Nevertheless I felt guilty—and hot. I don't suppose my hair was artistically barbered that night—I rather guess Mother had used the shears—and I can believe that I looked the half-wild colt I was; but there was no call for that youth to direct attention to my unavoidable shagginess.

I don't think the tree had many candles, and I don't remember that it glittered with golden apples. But it was loaded with presents, and the girls coming and going clothed in bright garments made me forget my own looks—I think they made me forget to remove my overcoat, which was a sodden thing of poor cut and worse quality. I think I must have stood agape for nearly two hours listening to the songs, noting every motion of Adoniram Burtch and Asa Walker as they directed the ceremonies and prepared the way for the great event—that is to say, for the coming of Santa Claus himself.

A furious jingling of bells, a loud voice outside, the lifting of a window, the nearer clash of bells, and the dear old saint appeared (in the person of Stephen Bartle) clothed in a red robe, a belt of sleigh bells, and a long white beard. The children cried out, "Oh!" The girls tittered and shrieked with excitement, and the boys laughed and clapped their hands. Then "Sandy" made a little speech about being glad to see us all, but as he had many other places to visit, and as there were a great many presents to distribute, he guessed he'd have to ask some of the many pretty girls to help him. So he called upon Betty Burtch and Hattie Knapp—and I for one admired his taste, for they were the most popular maids of the school.

They came up blushing, and a little bewildered by the blaze of publicity thus blown upon them. But their native dignity asserted itself, and the distribution of the presents began. I have a notion now that the fruit upon the tree was mostly bags of popcorn and "corny copias" of candy, but as my brother and I stood there that night and saw everybody, even the rowdiest boy, getting something we felt aggrieved and rebellious. We forgot that we had come from afar—we only knew that we were being left out.

But suddenly, in the midst of our gloom, my brother's name was called, and a lovely girl with a gentle smile handed him a bag of popcorn. My heart glowed with gratitude. Somebody had thought of us; and when she came to me, saying sweetly, "Here's something for you," I had not words to thank her. This happened nearly forty years ago,

but her smile, her outstretched hand, her sympathetic eyes are vividly before me as I write. She was sorry for the shock-headed boy who stood against the wall, and her pity made the little box of candy a casket of pearls. The fact that I swallowed the jewels on the road home does not take from the reality of my adoration.

At last I had to take my final glimpse of that wondrous tree, and I well remember the walk home. My brother and I traveled in wordless companionship. The moon was sinking toward the west, and the snow crust gleamed with a million fairy lamps. The sentinel watchdogs barked from lonely farmhouses, and the wolves answered from the ridges. Now and then sleighs passed us with lovers sitting two and two, and the bells on their horses had the remote music of romance to us whose boots drummed like clogs of wood upon the icy road.

Our house was dark as we approached and entered it, but how deliciously warm it seemed after the pitiless wind! I confess we made straight for the cupboard for a mince pie, a doughnut and a bowl of milk!

As I write this there stands in my library a thick-branched, beautifully tapering fir tree covered with the gold and purple apples of Hesperides, together with crystal ice points, green and red and yellow candles, clusters of gilded grapes, wreaths of metallic frost, and glittering angels swinging in ecstasy; but I doubt if my children will ever know the keen pleasure (that is almost pain) which came to my brother and to me in those days when an orange was not a breakfast fruit, but a casket of incense and of spice, a message from the sunlands of the South.

That was our compensation—we brought to Christmas a keen appetite and empty hands. And the lesson of it all is, if we are seeking a lesson, that it is better to give to those who want than to those for whom "we ought to do something because they did something for us last year."

Hamlin Garland

The Witnesses

The Hummingbird

Stowaway in the fold
Of the Negro wiseman's cloak,
I came from Mozambique
Having endured fierce cold,

Wind, rain and lashing sand—
Yet I have come thus far
To harbor in His hand,
and whir, His personal star.

The Owl

More credulous than I, men hold me wise
Not for my hoot, but for my full-moon eyes.
They are my mask; I see through not a soul
But only mice to fill my beak and bowl.
Perched in the eaves, I let my dreams congeal.
Who are those kings? Why do the oxen kneel?

The Goat

Munching a battered bucket by the crèche
I feel absolved from human sins of flesh.
A horny lecher men would make of me,
And scapegoat for their own indignity.

You who defame me, you who shift your blames
Onto my back and rout me with hard names,
Come, let us kneel beside the barley-cart,
That He may choose which are the pure in heart.

The Sheep

My wool in clumps like moss,
My diamond eyes agleam
I bleat my sheepish praise.
A Magus cuffs me. Who cares
What sheep think of a Lamb of God?
Wherefore all men, ye dumb
Sheepmouthed blobs of flesh and blood, rejoice
That such a holy babe will cry
Not with a bleat, but with a human voice.

The Ox

Like an ark unsettled from its Ararat
I rise, move to and fro,
One yellow eye on the Child.

So old I drool. My underwater eyes
Blink in distrust; can He be infinite
Who lies like daisies on a heap of straw?

Fumes circle in the stall
Where shaghaired Joseph, old a man
as I am ox, stands guard,
Among the easy beasts.
The weary Virgin lying in
And the old ox amovering along.

X. J. Kennedy

The Legend of the Camel

Camels look so haughty and sagacious. As least that's what I thought when I stopped on the north rim of the Sahara and watched a caravan plod sedately past our motor cars. We were making one of the earliest motor crossings of the Great Desert and as I watched the slow, steady, almost relentless movement of the camels, I actually felt apprehensive about our specially built desert cars.

At that time few of us doubted the legends about camels. Noble beasts, they knew the desert! Unhurried, they had carried the commerce of the Dark Continent for centuries, crossed trackless wastes without food. They drank less water than many other animals and could store up extra water in their humps and stomachs for anticipated drought. They could even outrun the swiftest horse. The romantics claimed that if the camel's master got lost in a sand storm, his loving beast would guide him home. Their broad spongy foot structure, we had been told, was especially adapted to negotiate the sandy world of deserts. Their great endurance shamed all other creatures.

Such were the "truths" about the camel. Six months later, after intimate daily contact with the beasts, including nearly 1,000 miles of travel on their backs, some of the legends crumbled. Each year since then I've gathered more information about camels, and the facts are stranger than fiction.

It was only a few days after we entered the Sahara that the first camel legend was shattered. We failed to reach our destination before dark one night and lost the trail for our cars. After an hour we were rescued by two men on horseback, who guided us over the sand to the oasis.

"Why did you ride out on horseback?" I asked our rescuers. "Aren't there any camels at this oasis?"

"Oh, yes, there are camels," they replied, "but horses can travel faster over sand than camels can. Then, too, if we got lost, we could let the horses have rein. They would

A camel can look haughty even when its winter coat appears to be coming apart at the seams. Spring shedding leaves enough fur to protect it from the hot summer sun.

bring us back to the stable, but a camel hasn't that much sense."

Later I used a white riding camel to cross the Western Erg. It stumbled and floundered in the sand like a wallowing ship on a storm-tossed sea. It is true that it has a spongy foot structure which spreads a little under its weight. But in spite of that, it negotiated the Sahara sands less easily and rapidly than the hard-hoofed horses of our escort. Camels trained in the sand areas did better than those brought up on the plains, but none of them did as well as the horses. On rocky and gravelly plains, which are far more common than sand areas in the deserts of the world, the camels' feet are often so badly cut that they have to be patched with pieces of leather sewn to them.

Apparently it is more common for a camel to get lost itself than to rescue a lost master. Among the great herds in the Syrian Desert the Bedouins say that a camel which finds a particularly attractive patch of pasture or a favorite fodder plant will often let the grazing herd move on without noticing. By night it has lost the herd and runs around moaning. Observers say that camels seem to lack entirely the sense of smell or the natural instinct that might enable them to find their herd.

The herdsmen can't leave their charges for long or others, too, would get lost. When they return to camp in the evening, one who has lost a camel goes through the whole encampment singing his special herd song. If the lost camel has joined another herd and hears the song of its herdsman it may walk toward him. In any case, if a lost camel is found, it is invariably the result of the herdsmen's search, not of any sixth sense belonging to the camel.

In books on the desert, statements about the loads a camel can carry, the speed it can travel, and the distance it can cover in a given period vary widely. Actually, loads vary from 200 pounds per camel to 1,200 according to the season, the frequency of water holes on the line of march, the length of the journey, and the physical condition of the animals.

Camels introduced into the southwestern United States in 1856 could carry 1,000-pound loads and travel 30 or 40 miles per day without water for six to ten days in winter. However, these camels were the biggest and strongest animals that could be found in the eastern Mediterranean and that southwestern vegetation, although inedible for horses and mules, was luxuriant camel fodder.

Caravans of The American Museum of Natural History in the Gobi of Mongolia used to load about 400 pounds per camel and travel 12 to 15 miles per day in June and July. Even under these circumstances, two or three camels were lost a season. Of course they had been on the trail since March and because the territory was unknown, all travel had to be in daylight. On regular well-known routes, the caravans would have traveled at night and let the camels feed by day.

There are records of camel riders in emergencies who covered 50 miles in a day and even 250 miles in five days, but these are exceptional cases and usually represent winter journeys. Five miles per hour is a good pace for a riding camel in the Sahara. The average speed for caravans is 2½ miles per hour, and a five- or six-hour day gives the animals time to rest and forage.

Unfortunately, there are no official racing records or radio sportcasters to settle arguments on camel speeds, loads, or distances traveled. Sahara military men will argue that in a race between horse and camel, the camel wins if the distance is long enough, the horse on a short course. Personally, I think it depends also on the individual horse and camel. When the Bedouins of the Syrian desert went on raids, they held the camels in reserve and used horses for the initial surprise. This seems to indicate agreement with the Saharan belief that horses are faster on a short distance.

Although camels are often given credit for great endurance, you will find that caravan owners in the Sahara, Arabian, or Gobi deserts are most reluctant to load their animals heavily. Left to their own time, they travel at a very leisurely pace and rest whenever they find a little pasture. In the Sahara, each member of the camel corps must own two riding camels, one ready for use and one to keep at pasture. They say, in fact, a camel is the most fragile of domestic animals. It either gets a six-month furlough every year or dies to spite you.

Perhaps that is where the expression, "the straw that broke the camel's back," started. This is about the only camel legend with some truth in it. The creatures go and go and finally collapse—the "one-hoss shay" of the animal kingdom.

Legends of the camel and its water-drinking habits were the most recent to give way to facts. The Drs. Schmidt-Nielsen, husband-and-wife team of physiologists, have investigated these legends with results that only controlled scientific experiments can give. For several months they worked with camels in the Sahara, weighing them before and after drinking. They kept records of body temperature, tested blood and body fluids, and finally dissected dead animals. Their findings explain the camel's way of life and account for the wide variation among the claims made about the beasts.

Camels do not store up water. They only replace the quantity lost since the last drink. The Schmidt-Nielsens have records of one camel which drank over 27 gallons of water in ten minutes, nearly one-third of its own weight. In less than 48 hours, this water was evenly distributed to restore blood, body fluids, and cells to their normal water balance. The Schmidt-Nielsens studies also showed that unless it was dehydrated, the camel would not drink at all, even if it had gone for months without drinking.

In Egypt the camel can go for three or four months without drinking between November and April if it is in lush pasture where the vegetation is kept green by dew and showers. If it is on dry feed, the camel will get thirsty in a couple of weeks, even during January. It is evident, then, that the length of time a camel can go without drinking is much affected by the time of year, force of wind, heat in the air, intensity of the sunlight, amount of reflected heat from the desert floor, dryness of the feed, kind of feed, weight of the load carried, speed the animal

Camels freighting precious salt on their backs trek across the sands of North Africa's Tenere Desert with Tuareg tribesmen following centuries-old routes.

travels, and the hours spent in travel each day. These same conditions bear on the need for water in human beings, horses, and donkeys. Nevertheless, it is the camel that can best adjust to the extremes of the desert.

Like man, the camel must keep its body temperature within certain bounds through perspiration, but for the camel there is more leeway. Its temperature in the morning may go as low as 93° and rise in the daytime heat to more than 104°, representing a daily range of 12 degrees. Man must keep his temperature within a degree or so of 98.6°. The camel has another advantage, too: it can tolerate dehydration to more than 30% of its body weight, while man is in trouble when he has lost water equal to 10% or 12% of his weight.

Dehydration does not impair the camel's appetite, so it keeps eating and restoring its energy. Its woolly coat keeps out the heat of direct sunlight, reflected heat from the sand, and heat in the surrounding air. The wool also allows sweat to evaporate slowly and so cool its body more efficiently. Its wide temperature range is one of the camel's most important assets. This is because heat moves faster on a steep gradient than on a slow one. Air at 110° gives heat faster to a body at 98.6° than one at 104°. So, the camel doesn't get as much heat from its environment as man would because its body temperature is closer to the temperature of the desert air to start with. Also, when its temperature is rising, the camel is storing heat for the cool night. So, it is not storage of extra water that allows the camel to go without drinking, but rather its tolerance of great dehydration and its wide range of body temperature.

The Schmidt-Nielsens found that the camel's stomach and rumen sacs, which desert legend credits with water storage, do contain liquid and sometimes solid food. This liquid, however, has as much salt in it as the blood or other body fluids. Furthermore, the capacity of the little sacs is insignificant compared to the amount of water the camel needs.

No doubt there is some truth in the stories of drinking the contents of camel stomachs in desert emergencies. As recently as 1920 various Bedouins of Syria had done exactly that. Unappetizing as these normal juices must have been, they did restore the energy and prolong the lives of these dehydrated men. But they did not represent extra or stored water.

There is no water in the camel's hump, either. It is fat, stored energy, like the hump on Brahma cattle now so common in the southern United States. Some students have reasoned that when the fat of the camel's hump is utilized it produces more than its weight in water and that the hump, therefore, does indirectly store water. The physiologists disproved this. They have shown that it takes a lot of oxygen to combine with fat and transform it into usable energy. Since oxygen comes through the lungs, this necessitates increased breathing and, consequently, more moisture evaporated in the exhaled breath. As a result, extra water produced from metabolized fat escapes from the body. Even though the hump isn't a water tank, it is quite a remarkable feature: a light, easily carried form of energy that keeps the camel supplied after the feed bag is empty or the pasture dried up.

The camel did make history in Africa by making commerce feasible between white North Africa and black Central Africa. It almost made history in America but was superseded too quickly by the railroads. It may still make agricultural history in the Near East as a meat animal because it can thrive on little water and on desert plants that few other animals will eat.

The camel has taught me the basic principles of desert living: keep out heat by wearing clothes that cover the body and still let sweat evaporate efficiently; travel slowly to keep down the production of body heat; drink water when you are thirsty to stay within safe water balance limits; take long vacations to fatten up and restore energy.

I still don't like the critters. Their stare is haughty, their manner insolent. They complain constantly, they don't know the way home, and their breath smells. But although they are a holdover from the zoological past, they get a lot of mileage on a gallon of water and have a most efficient heat-control system!

Alonzo W. Pond

My Side of the Mountain

In this modern adventure tale, Sam Gribley has run away from his tenement home in New York City to prove to his sailor father that he can live off the land for a year. In a remote gorge in the Catskill Mountains 14-year-old Sam has made a snug den for himself inside the hollow trunk of a huge hemlock tree. Smoke from his tiny stone fireplace chimney goes out through a knothole. One deerskin covers the doorway, another his bed.

By autumn Sam has squirreled away in a nearby hollow tree dried apples, herbs, nuts, acorns, tubers, smoked fish and venison. His only companion is a falcon that he has tamed and named Frightful.

In the excerpt that follows, Sam tells how he survived Nature's sternest test—the icy grip of winter.

With Christmas over, the winter became serious. Outside my cozy tree house the snow deepened, the wind blew, the temperatures dropped. Never had humanity seemed so far away as it did in those cold still months of January, February, and March. I wandered the snowy crags, I slept, ate, played my reed whistle, and talked to Frightful. I was in excellent condition. Not a cold, not a sniffle, not a moment of fatigue. I enjoyed the feeling that I could eat, sleep and be warm, and outwit the storms that blasted the mountains and the subzero temperatures that numbed them.

I plowed through drifts and stamped paths until it occurred to me that I had all the materials to make snowshoes—young ash saplings, deer hide, and a pen knife. When I first walked in them, I tripped on my toes and fell, but by the end of the first day I could walk from my tree to the gorge in half the time.

I lived close to the weather. It is surprising how you watch it when you live in it. Not a cloud passed unnoticed, not a wind blew untested. I knew the moods of the storms, where they came from, their shapes and colors.

When the sun shone, I took Frightful to the meadow and we slid down the mountain on my snapping-turtle-shell sled. When the winds changed and the air smelled like snow, I would stay in my tree, because I had gotten lost in a blizzard one afternoon and had had to hole up in a rock ledge until I could see where I was going. That taught me to stay home when the air said "snow."

I usually came home at night with the nuthatch that roosted in a nearby sapling. When you don't have a newspaper or radio to give you weather bulletins, watch the birds and animals. They can tell when a storm is coming. I called the nuthatch "Barometer," and when he holed up, I holed up, lit my turtleshell lamp that I kept filled with deer fat with a strip of my trousers for a wick, and sat by my fire.

There is no such thing as a "still winter night." Not only are many animals running around in the creaking cold, but the trees cry out and limbs snap and fall, and the wind gets caught in a ravine and screams until it dies. One noisy night I wrote in my diary:

"There is somebody in my bedroom. I can hear small exchanges of greetings and little feet moving up the wall. By the time I get to my light all is quiet."

Next day

"There was something in my room last night; a small tunnel leads out from my door into the snow. I would say, mouse."

That night

"I got a fast light before the visitor could get to the door. It was a mouse—a perfect little white-footed deer mouse with enormous black eyes and tidy white feet. I handed him a nut meat. He took it in his fragile paws, stuffed it

into his cheek, flipped, and went out his secret tunnel. No doubt the tunnel leads right over to my store tree, and this fellow is having a fat winter."

There were no raccoons or skunks about in the snow, but the mice, the weasels, the mink, the foxes, the shrews, the cottontail rabbits were all busier than Coney Island in July. Their tracks were all over the mountain, and their activities ranged from catching each other to hauling various materials back to their dens and burrows for more insulation.

By day the birds were a-wing. They got up late, after I did, and would call to each other before hunting.

On January 8, I stirred up my fire and wrote in my birchbark diary:

"I took Frightful out today. We went over to the meadow to catch a rabbit for her; as we passed one of the hemlocks near the edge of the grove, she pulled her feathers to her body and looked alarmed. I tried to find out what had frightened her, but saw nothing.

"On the way back we passed the same tree and I noticed an owl pellet in the snow. I looked up, and there it was, a great horned owl. I hit the tree and he flew off. Those great wings— they must have been five feet across—beat the wind, but there was no sound. It is really very special to have a great horned owl for a neighbor because he is such a wilderness bird."

One day I did not notice a gray sheet of cloud sneaking up the mountain from the northwest. It covered the sun suddenly. I whistled for Frightful, and started back to the tree. We holed up just as Barometer flew home, and it was none too soon. It drizzled, it misted, it sprinkled, and finally it froze. The deerhide door grew stiff with ice as darkness came.

I made a fire, my tree room warmed, and I puttered around. When I tried to open the deerskin door, it wouldn't budge. I kicked it. It gave a little, cracking like china, and I realized that I was going to be iced in if I didn't keep that door open.

I finally got it open. There must have been an inch and a half of ice on it. I ate my supper and went to bed.

I awoke twice and kicked open the door. Then I fell into a sound sleep that lasted hours beyond my usual rising time. I had overslept, I discovered, because none of the morning sounds of the forest could penetrate my glass house to awaken me. I was sealed in. The first thing I did was try to open the door; I chipped and kicked and managed to peep out to see what had happened. Now, I have seen ice storms, and I know they can be shiny and glassy and treacherous, but this was something else. There were sheets of ice binding the aspens to earth and cementing the tops of the hemlocks in arches. It was inches thick! Frightful winged out of the door and flew to a limb, where she tried to perch. She slipped, dropped to the ground, and skidded on her wings and undercoverts to a low spot where she stopped.

I laughed at her, and then I came out and took a step. I landed with an explosion on my seat. The jolt splintered the ice and sent glass-covered limbs clattering to earth like a shopful of shattering crystal. As I sat there, not daring to move because I hurt, I heard an enormous explosion. It was followed by splintering and clattering and smashing. A maple at the edge of the meadow had been torn apart by the weight of ice on its limbs. I feared now for my tree—the ice was too heavy to bear. I sort of swam back into my tree, listening to trees being ripped apart all over the mountain. It was a fearful and dreadful sound. I lit a fire, ate smoked fish and dried apples, and went out again. I saw my iron wagon axle iced against a tree, and crawled to it. I de-iced it with the butt of my ax, and used it for a cane. I would stab it into the ground and inch along. I fell a couple of times but not as hard as that first.

The next day I heard the drip, drip begin, and by evening some of the trees had dumped their loads and were slowly lifting themselves to their feet, so to speak. Three days later, the forest arose, the ice melted, and for about a day or so we had warm, glorious weather.

The mountain was a mess. Broken trees, fallen limbs were everywhere. The birds were starved, and many had died.

Frightful ate old frozen muskrat during those days. We couldn't kick up a live rabbit or even a mouse. They were in the snow under the ice, waiting it out. I suppose the mice went right on tunneling to the grasses and the mosses and had no trouble staying alive, but I did wonder how The Baron Weasel was doing. I needn't have. He appeared after the ice storm, looking sleek and pleased with himself. I think he dined royally on the many dying animals and birds. That Baron!

After the ice storm came more snow. I still had food, but all the fresh frozen venison was gone, and most of the bulbs and tubers. I longed for just a simple dandelion green.

Toward the end of January I began to feel tired, and my elbows and knees were a little stiff. This worried me. I figured it was due to some vitamin I wasn't getting, but I couldn't remember which vitamin it was or even where I would find it if I could remember it.

One morning my nose bled. It frightened me a bit, and I wondered if I shouldn't give up and hike down to the village to the library and reread the material on vitamins. It didn't last long, however, so I figured it wasn't too serious. I decided I would last until the greens came to the land.

On that same day Frightful caught a rabbit in the meadow. As I cleaned it, the liver suddenly looked so tempting that I could hardly wait to cook it. For the next week, I really craved liver and took

them from her with hunger. The tiredness ended, the bones stopped aching and I had no more nosebleeds. Hunger is a funny thing. It has a kind of intelligence all its own. I ate fresh rabbit liver almost every day until the first plants emerged, and I never had any more trouble. I have looked up vitamins since. I am not surprised to find that liver is rich in vitamin C. So are citrus fruits and green vegetables, but liver was the only available source—and on liver I stuffed, without knowing why.

On February 6, I wrote in my diary:

"The deer have pressed in all around me. They are hungry. Apparently they stamp out yards in the valleys where they feed during the dawn and dusk, but many of them climb back to my hemlock grove to hide and sleep for the day. They manage the deep snows so effortlessly on those slender hooves."

I got to worrying about the deer, and for many days I climbed trees and cut down tender limbs for them. At first only two came, then five, and soon I had a ring of white-tailed deer, waiting at my tree at twilight. I was astonished to see this herd grow, and wondered what signals they used to inform each other of my services. Did they smell fatter? Look more contented? Somehow they were able to tell their friends that there was a free lunch on my side of the mountain, and more and more arrived.

Three nights later they all disappeared. Not one deer came for limbs. I looked down the valley, and in the dim light could see the open earth on the land below. The deer could forage again. Spring was coming to the land! My heart beat faster. I think I was trembling. The valley also blurred. The only thing that can do that is tears, so I guess I was crying.

That night the great horned owls boomed out across the land. My notes read:

"February 10

"I think the great horned owls have eggs! The mountain is white, the wind blows, the snow is hard packed, but spring is beginning in the hollow in the maple. I will climb it tomorrow.

"February 12

"Yes, yes, yes, yes. It is spring in the maple. Two great horned owl eggs lie in the cavity in the broken top of the tree. They were warm to my touch. Eggs in the snow. Now isn't that wonderful? I didn't stay long, for it is bitter weather and I wanted the female to return immediately. I climbed down, and as I ran off toward my tree I saw her drift on muffled wings as she went back to her work. I crawled through the tunnel of ice that leads to my tree, and spent the evening whittling and thinking about the owl high in the forest with the first new life of the spring."

And so with the disappearance of the deer, the hoot of the owl, the cold land began to create new life. Spring is terribly exciting when you are living right in it. I was hungry for green vegetables, and that night as I went off to sleep, I thought of the pokeweeds, the dandelions, the spring beauties that would soon be pressing up from the earth.

Jean George

Index

Picture Credits

Cover: Deer, David Alan Harvey/Woodfin Camp, Inc. Pages 2-3: Hauling Christmas tree home, Richard W. Brown. 4-5: " Con tents," illustrations by Bob Hynes.

SPRING

Pages 6-7: Greening hilltop, Richard W. Brown. 8-9: Facsimile pages from *The Country Diary of an Edwardian Lady* by Edith Holden. Copyright © 1977 by Webb and Bower Ltd. Reprinted by permission of Holt, Rinehart and Winston, Publishers. 11: Ibis, Wendell Metzen. 12-13: Birds and eggs, Hal H. Harrison. 14: Indian egg dancer, *Indien in Wort und Bild* by Emil Schlagintweit, Leipzig, 1880. 15: "Egg Running in Switzerland," courtesy of the Swiss National Library, Bern. 16: Ukrainian eggs, *Eggs Beautiful: How to Make Ukrainian Easter Eggs* by Johanna Luciow, Ann Kmit, and Loretta Luciow. 17: Easter cards, Hallmark Historical Collection. 18: Egg butterflies, Robert L. Dunne (NWF). 19: Egg bunny, Mel Baughman (NWF). Egg bird, Mel Baughman (NWF). 20: Daffodils, Thase Daniel. 21: Skunk, Carson Baldwin, Jr. Skunk cabbage, Gene C. Frazier. Mourning cloak butterfly, L. West. Red fox, Les Blacklock. 22: Peacock, Malcolm Gilson/TOM STACK & ASSOCIATES. 23: Elk, C. Allan Morgan. Sarus cranes, M. P. Kahl. 24: Cattle egrets, William J. Weber. Snails, Lois Cox. Frogs, E. S. Ross. 25: Butterflies, Kjell B. Sandved. Dragonflies, Kjell B. Sandved. 26: Flamingos, M. P. Kahl. Possums, Richard S. Diego. 27: Dall sheep, Stephen J. Krasemann. 29: Dewdrops, Hans Pfletschinger from Peter Arnold, Inc. 30-31: Wild flowers, illustrations by Arthur J. Anderson. 32-33: Wildflower garden, Sonja Bullaty. 34: Flying kite, Leah Bendavid-Val (NWF). 35-36: Making kite, Leah Bendavid-Val (NWF). 37: Kite pattern by Janice Hawkins (NWF), adapted from a design by Paul Garber, Historian Emeritus, National Air and Space Museum, Smithsonian Institution.

SUMMER

Pages 38-39: Beach, Entheos. 40-41: Facsimile pages from *The Country Diary of an Edwardian Lady* by Edith Holden. Copyright © 1977 by Webb and Bower Ltd. Reprinted by permission of Holt, Rinehart and Winston, Publishers. 42: Fireworks, Marvin Ickow/Bruce Coleman, Inc. 45: Bald eagle nest, Jeff Foott. 46: Bald eagle, Jeff Foott/Bruce Coleman, Inc. 47: Bald eagle, Robert Burr Smith. 48-49: Detail from *Threshing Wheat*, by Thomas Hart Benton, Permanent Collection, Sheldon Swope Art Gallery, Terre Haute, Indiana. 50: Children picking blueberries, Clyde H. Smith. 51: Blueberries, L. West/Photo Researchers. 52-53: Fishing, Wendell Metzen. 54: 17-Mile Drive, Fred Ragsdale. 55: Grand Canyon, Shelly Grossman/Woodfin Camp & Associates. Mojave Desert, David Muench. 56: Niagara Falls, J. Messerschmidt/Bruce Coleman, Inc. 56-57: Cape Cod, Clyde H. Smith. Blue Ridge Mountains, Sonja Bullaty. 57: Cape Hatteras, Bruce Roberts. Old Man of the Mountains, Clyde H. Smith. 58: Old Faithful, EARTH SCENES/© Alan G. Nelson. Monument Valley, Josef Muench Photo. Painted Desert, Shelly Grossman/Woodfin Camp & Associates. Olympic National Park, Keith Gunnar/Bruce Coleman, Inc. 59: Devil's Tower, EARTH SCENES/© Breck P. Kent. 61: Sea's edge, David Muench. 62: Shells, Russ Kinne. 63: Shelling, Entheos. 65: "Jody and the Flutter-Mill," N. C. Wyeth. Copyright © 1939 by Charles Scrib-

Text Credits

The Editors wish to thank the publishers listed below for permission to present the following selections:

SPRING

"A Diary For All Seasons" (p. 8), from *The Country Diary of an Edwardian Lady* by Edith Holden. Copyright © 1977 by Webb and Bower Ltd. Reprinted by permission of Holt, Rinehart and Winston, Publishers.

"Of Spring and an Egg" (p. 10), reprinted with permission from the April 1966 *Reader's Digest*. Copyright © 1966 by The Reader's Digest Association, Inc.

"Easter Egg Zoo" (p. 18), egg butterflies adapted from the March 1967 issue of *Family Circle Magazine*. Copyright © 1967 THE FAMILY CIRCLE, INC. All rights reserved. Egg bird from *Easter Eggs for Everyone* by Evelyn Coskey. Copyright © 1973 by Abingdon Press. Used by permission.

"Impatient Spring" (p. 20), reprinted with permission from the February 1969 *Reader's Digest* and Ronald Rood. Originally from *Vermont Life* (Spring '68), copyright © by Vermont Life Magazine.

"April Showers" (p. 28), reprinted with permission from the April 1962 *Reader's Digest*. Copyright © 1962 by The Reader's Digest Association, Inc.

"Gardening With Wild Flowers" (p. 30), copyright 1970 by the National Wildlife Federation. Reprinted from the April/May issue of *National Wildlife* Magazine.

"How To Make a Butterfly Kite" (p. 34), condensed from instructions by Paul Garber, Historian Emeritus, National Air and Space Museum, Smithsonian Institution.

SUMMER

"Country Diary" (p. 40), from *The Country Diary of an Edwardian Lady* by Edith Holden. Copyright © 1977 by Webb and Bower Ltd. Reprinted by permission of Holt, Rinehart and Winston, Publishers.

"The Glorious Fourth" (p. 43), "America for Me" by Henry van Dyke is reprinted from *The Poems of Henry van Dyke* with the permission of Charles Scribner's Sons. Copyright 1911 Charles Scribner's Sons. "The Gift Outright" from *The Poetry of Robert Frost* edited by Edward Connery Lathem. Copyright 1942 by Robert Frost. Copyright 1969 by Holt, Rinehart and Winston. Copyright 1970 by Lesley Frost Ballantine. Reprinted by permission of Holt, Rinehart and Winston, Publishers. "Fireworks" from *The Blackbird in the Lilac* by James Reeves, published by Oxford University Press (1952). Reprinted by permission of the publisher.

"Our National Bird" (p. 44), a condensation of a portion of Chapter 1, "The National Bird," from *Autumn of the Eagle* by George Laycock is reprinted with the permission of Charles Scribner's Sons. Copyright © 1973 George Laycock.

"Threshing Time" (p. 48), a condensation of "Threshing Time" by Earl Bihlmeyer which appeared in the July 1976 *Gourmet* magazine, is reprinted with permission of *Gourmet* and Earl Bihlmeyer.

"Blueberry Summer" (p. 50), copyright © 1976 by The Condé Nast Publications Inc.

"Why Presidents Fish" (p. 52), excerpts from *Fishing For Fun And To Wash Your Soul*, by Herbert Hoover. Copyright © 1963 by Herbert Hoover. Reprinted by permission of Random House, Inc.

"Journey Into Summer" (p. 54), from *Journey Into Summer* by Edwin Way Teale. Reprinted by permission of Dodd, Mead & Company.

"Life at the Edge of the Sea" (p. 60), from "The Marginal World" in *The Edge of the Sea* by Rachel Carson. Copyright 1955 by Rachel L. Carson. Reprinted by permission of Houghton Mifflin Company.

"Hunting Treasure on the Beach" (p. 62), copyright 1969 by the National Wildlife Federation. Reprinted from the January issue of *Ranger Rick's Nature Magazine*.

"Jody and the Flutter-Mill" (p. 64), excerpt from the text and one illustration by N. C. Wyeth from *The Yearling* by Marjorie Kinnan Rawlings are reprinted with the permission of Charles Scribner's Sons. Text copyright 1938 Marjorie Kinnan Rawlings. Illustration copyright 1939 Charles Scribner's Sons.

"Summer Symphony" (p. 68), copyright 1977 by the National Wildlife Federation. Reprinted from the July issue of *Ranger Rick's Nature Magazine*.

"Nature's Nightlight" (p. 70), copyright 1969 by the National Wildlife Federation. Reprinted from the July issue of *Ranger Rick's Nature Magazine*.

AUTUMN

"Country Diary" (p. 74), from *The Country Diary of an Edwardian Lady* by Edith Holden. Copyright © 1977 by Webb and Bower Ltd. Reprinted by permission of Holt, Rinehart and Winston, Publishers.

"Migration" (p. 76), condensed from *Defenders* magazine. Copyright 1977, Defenders of Wildlife, 1244 Nineteenth Street,

ner's Sons. 68: "Summer Symphony," illustration by Cyndy Szekeres. 69: Insect anatomy, diagrams by Arabelle Wheatley. 70: Glowing firefly, Ivan Polunin. Firefly tree, Ivan Polunin. Firefly on leaf, E. S. Ross.

AUTUMN

Pages 72-73: Autumn scene, Richard W. Brown. 74-75: Facsimile pages from *The Country Diary of an Edwardian Lady* by Edith Holden. Copyright © 1977 by Webb and Bower Ltd. Reprinted by permission of Holt, Rinehart and Winston, Publishers. 77: Geese, Clyde H. Smith. 78-79: Salmon, Rollie Ostermick. 79: Monarch butterflies, Tom McHugh/Photo Researchers. 80: Army ants, ANIMALS ANIMALS/© Raymond A. Mendez. 81: Caribou, George W. Calef. 82-85: "Mr. Crow Takes a Wife," illustrations by Cyndy Szekeres. 86: Fall leaves, John Shaw. 86-87: Fall scenic, Zig Leszczyzynski. 87: Fall scene, Dick Smith. Leaf close-up, Barbara G. Hallowell. Fall scene, David Muench. 88: Hickory trees, Ned Smith. 89: Beechnuts, Ned Smith. Pecans, Ned Smith. 90: Black walnuts, Ned Smith. 91: Hazelnuts, Ned Smith. 92-93: Bee line, reprinted with permission of *Ford Times* magazine, Ford Motor Company. 95: Smoking bee tree, reprinted with permission of *Ford Times* magazine, Ford Motor Company. 96-97: Detail from

Grandma Moses (1860-1961): *Halloween.* Copyright © 1955, Grandma Moses Properties, Inc., New York. 98-99: *Cider Making on Long Island*, by William Davis, New York State Historical Association, Cooperstown. 100: Apples, courtesy of Reader's Digest Association, Inc. 101: Cider making, Hanson Carroll. 102: *American Field Sports. A Chance for Both Barrels*, by Currier and Ives, Harry T. Peters Collection, Museum of the City of New York. 104: Turkey, Leonard Lee Rue III. 107: Thanksgiving games and feast, Plimoth Plantation.

WINTER

Pages 108-109: Winter Scenic, Clyde H. Smith. 110-111: Facsimile pages from *The Country Diary of an Edwardian Lady* by Edith Holden. Copyright © 1977 by Webb and Bower Ltd. Reprinted by permission of Holt, Rinehart and Winston, Publishers. 112-113: Raccoon, Olive Glasgow. 113: Little brown bats, Stephen J. Krasemann. Marmot, Jeff Foott/Bruce Coleman, Inc. 114: Coyote, Jon Cates. Snowy owl, Gary Meszaros. 115: Wolves, Tom McHugh/Photo Researchers. Puma, Maurice Hornocker. Weasel, Franz J. Camenzind. 116: Bear, Rollie Ostermick. 116-117: Beaver, Harry Engels. 117: Deer, Les Blacklock. Red Squirrel, Stephen J. Krasemann. Bison, Len Rue, Jr./Bruce Coleman, Inc. 118-119: *Winter Sports-Pick-*

erel Fishing, by Currier and Ives, Harry T. Peters Collection, Museum of the City of New York. 120: Christmas bird count, Kent and Donna Dannen. Cardinal, George H. Harrison. 121: Snowy egret, Peter L. Vila. Goldfinch, Thase Daniel/Bruce Coleman, Inc. 122: Decorations, illustrations by Janice Hawkins (NWF), based on drawings in *The Trees of Christmas* by Edna Metcalfe. 123: Tree, from *The Trees of Christmas* by Edna Metcalfe. Copyright © 1969 by Abingdon Press. Reprinted by permission. 124-125: Birds, illustrations by Marilyn Hafner. 127: Christmas trees, Richard W. Brown. 128-129: "The Plants of Christmas," illustrations by Chuck Ripper. 130: Natural tree decorations, Barbara G. Hallowell. 131: Tree, Barbara G. Hallowell. Decorations, Barbara G. Hallowell. 132-133: "Christmas Critters," created by Donna Miller. 134: Bread wreath, Leah Bendavid-Val (NWF). 135: Cookie wreath, Leah Bendavid-Val (NWF). 136-139: From *The Father Christmas Letters* by J. R. R. Tolkien. Copyright © George Allen & Unwin (Publishers) Ltd. 1976. Reprinted by permission of Houghton Mifflin Company. 140-141: Christmas party, illustration by Susan Davis. 144-145: "The Witnesses," illustration by Jo Anna Poehlmann. 146-147: Camel, E. Turri/Bruce Coleman, Inc. 149: Camels, Victor Englebert. 150-154: "My Side of the Mountain," illustrations by Ted Lewin.

N.W., Washington, D.C. 20036.

"Mr. Crow Takes a Wife" (p. 82), reprinted with permission of Macmillan Publishing Co., Inc. from *Beyond the Clapping Mountains, Eskimo Stories from Alaska* by Charles E. Gillham. Copyright 1943 by Macmillan Publishing Co., Inc. Renewed 1971 by Virginia L. Gillham, Edward Gillham and Mrs. John A. Cezek.

"Bright Passage" (p. 86), copyright 1977 by the National Wildlife Federation. Reprinted from the October/November issue of *National Wildlife* Magazine.

"The Sweetest Meat Grows on Trees" (p. 88), copyright 1972 by the National Wildlife Federation. Condensed from the October/November issue of *National Wildlife* Magazine. "Nut Dressing" recipe from *Anne Marie's Cookingschool Cook Book*. Copyright © 1974 by Anne Marie Huste. Reprinted by permission of Houghton Mifflin Company. Condensed version of "Nut Casserole" Copyright © 1972 by Jean Hewitt. Reprinted by permission of Times Books from THE NEW YORK TIMES NATURAL COOKBOOK by Jean Hewitt. "Pralines," "Chestnut Stuffing Chimney Hill," "Wonderful Walnut Pie Crust," "Hickory-Nut Brittle," "Filbert and Fruit Candy" recipes from *The How to Grow and Cook It Book of Vegetables, Herbs, Fruits, and Nuts* by Jacqueline Heriteau. Copyright © 1970 by Jacqueline Heriteau. Copyright under International and Pan-American Copyright Conventions. By permission of Hawthorn Books, Inc.

"The Day We Smoked the Bee Tree" (p. 92), from the September 1976 issue of *Ford Times* magazine. Reprinted with permission of the publisher, the Ford Motor Company.

"Hallowe'en" (p. 96), "This Is Hallowe'en" from *Child Life* magazine, October 1941. Copyright © 1941 by Rand McNally & Co., reassigned to Dorothy Brown Thompson. Used by permission. "Hallowe'en Indignation Meeting" reprinted by permission of Marga-

ret Fishback Antolini.

"Cider" (p. 98), copyright © 1975 by Evan Jones.

"Bringing Out the Beast" (p. 102), copyright © *The Washington Post.*

WINTER

"Country Diary" (p. 110), from *The Country Diary of an Edwardian Lady* by Edith Holden. Copyright © 1977 by Webb and Bower Ltd. Reprinted by permission of Holt, Rinehart and Winston, Publishers.

"Now the Animal World Goes to Sleep" (p. 112), from *If You Don't Mind My Saying So* (1964) by Joseph Wood Krutch. Copyright © 1959 by Joseph Wood Krutch. By permission of William Morrow & Company. Formerly published by William Sloane Assoc.

"O Come All Ye Bird Counters" (p. 120), excerpted from *Saturday Review*. Copyright © *Saturday Review*, 1972. All rights reserved.

"A Christmas Tree for the Birds" (p. 122), from *The Trees of Christmas* by Edna Metcalfe. Copyright © 1969 by Abingdon Press. Reprinted by permission.

"Recipes for the Birds" (p. 124), from *My Recipes Are for the Birds* by Irene Cosgrove. Illustrated by Ed Cosgrove. Copyright © 1975, 1976 by Irene E. Cosgrove and Ed Cosgrove. Condensed and reprinted by permission of Doubleday & Company, Inc.

"Christmas Trees" (p. 126), from *The Poetry of Robert Frost* edited by Edward Connery Lathem. Copyright 1916, © 1969 by Holt, Rinehart and Winston. Copyright 1944 by Robert Frost. Reprinted by permission of Holt, Rinehart and Winston, Publishers.

"The Plants of Christmas" (p. 128), reprinted by permission of Curtis Brown, Ltd. Text copyright © 1969 by Hal Borland.

"Christmas Critters" (p. 132), copyright

1968 by the National Wildlife Federation. Reprinted from the December issue of *Ranger Rick's Nature Magazine.*

"Delicious Holiday Wreaths" (p. 134), "Orange Coffee Braid" adapted from "Holiday Twist," *Seventeen* ® magazine. Copyright © 1973 by Triangle Communications, Inc. All rights reserved. "Sugar-Plum Cookies" adapted from *Seventeen* ® magazine. Copyright © 1966 by Triangle Communications, Inc. All rights reserved.

"The Father Christmas Letters" (p. 136), from *The Father Christmas Letters* by J. R. R. Tolkien. Copyright © George Allen & Unwin (Publishers) Ltd. 1976. Reprinted by permission of Houghton Mifflin Company.

"My First Christmas Tree" (p. 140), reprinted by permission of Constance Garland Doyle and Isabel Garland Lord.

"The Witnesses" (p. 144), reprinted by permission of X. J. Kennedy.

"The Legend of the Camel" (p. 146), reprinted with permission from *Natural History* magazine, May 1957. Copyright © The American Museum of Natural History 1957.

"My Side of the Mountain" (p. 150), from *My Side of the Mountain* by Jean George. Copyright © 1959 by Jean George. Reprinted by permission of the publishers, E. P. Dutton.

Library of Congress Cataloging in Publication Data

Main entry under title:

Wildlife's holiday album.

Includes index.

1. Nature—Literary collections. 2. Holidays—Literary collections. I. National Wildlife Federation.

PN6071.N3W55   500.9   78-56861

ISBN 0-912186-27-5

National
Wildlife
Federation

1412 16th St., N.W.
Washington, D.C. 20036

Dedicated to improving the quality of our environment
Thomas L. Kimball, Executive Vice President
J. A. Brownridge, Administrative Vice President
James D. Davis, Director, Book Development

Staff for this Book
Alma Deane MacConomy, Editor
Elizabeth Jones, Art Editor
Howard F. Robinson, Research Editor
Charles O. Hyman, Designer
Mel Baughman, Production and Printing
Janice Hawkins, Production Artist
Cathy Pelletier, Permissions Editor

Acknowledgments

The editors are especially grateful to David F. Robinson
for the way in which he captured the essence of this book
in the seasonal essays which introduce each section. He is
one of that exuberant company of essayists, poets and nov-
elists, artists and photographers, scientists, humorists,
diarists and chefs whose joy in the celebration of nature
and of holidays makes an anthology like this one possible.

The editorial staff also acknowledge with thanks the
day-to-day saving help of National Wildlife naturalists
Craig Tufts and Susan Ennett; wildlife biologist William
S. Clark; designer Mary Ann Smith; our fellow editors of
National and *International Wildlife* magazines and of
Ranger Rick's Nature Magazine; and the interest and
assistance of reference librarians at the Library of
Congress and the Fairfax (Virginia) Public Library.